Almshouses

Also by Brian Bailey

English Manor Houses
Stone Villages of England
The English Village Green
Churchyards of England and Wales

Almshouses

BRIAN BAILEY

ROBERT HALE · LONDON

Robert Hale Limited
Clerkenwell House
Clerkenwell Green
London EC1R OHT

British Library Cataloguing in Publication Data
Bailey, Brian J. (Brian John), 1934–
Almshouses.
1. England. Almshouses, to 1988
I. Title
363.5'8

ISBN 0-7090-3292-7

Set in Sabon by Rowland Phototypesetting Limited
Bury St Edmunds, Suffolk
Printed in Great Britain by
St Edmundsbury Press Limited, Bury St Edmunds, Suffolk
and bound by WBC Bookbinders Limited

Contents

Acknowledgements

I wish to express my thanks, first and foremost, to the many people, among both staff and residents of almshouses in various parts of England, who have shown me their premises and talked to me about them.

I am especially grateful, also, to Mr David Scott and Mrs Heather Greves of the National Association of Almshouses, for the trouble they went to in supplying information and answering my various questions.

Mr Ken Payne, General Secretary of the Durham Aged Miners' Housing Association, and Claire Nunns of the Dickens House Museum, kindly supplied information for which I am most grateful.

Finally, my thanks to all who have given me particular help with the illustrations for the book.

Introduction

I have attempted in this book to outline the development of the English almshouse, as both a social and an architectural phenomenon, from its medieval origins up to the present day. This has not been done before, previous books about almshouses, which are in any case few and far between, dealing principally with the architectural aspects of mainly medieval and Tudor foundations. The exception is Rotha Mary Clay's excellent 1909 volume (see the select bibliography) which dealt thoroughly with all aspects of charitable foundations, but only those of medieval origin.

The present book is not intended to cover *all* almshouses in England. There are around two and a half thousand groups of almshouses in this country, housing something approaching thirty thousand old people. Inevitably, the few hundred foundations mentioned here tend to be those of particular architectural merit or social and historical interest, at the expense of the small and humble foundations to be found in towns and villages throughout the land. But I have not ignored the latter altogether, and it is worth pointing out here that many of them were built with relatively greater generosity by their founders than some of the more visibly lavish buildings elsewhere. The widow's mite still deserves greater respect than the millionaire's loose change, particularly when the latter was given as an act of self-glorification.

A word may be necessary about usage. An 'almshouse', strictly speaking, is one dwelling, but as the word is interchangeable with 'hospital' in the earlier period, some confusion of singular and plural is inevitable, and I have used 'almshouse' and 'almshouses' freely as seemed relevant in each instance.

List of Illustrations

The Beaufort Tower, Hospital of St Cross, Winchester

1 Pity or Piety? The Medieval Hospital

The oldest almshouse surviving in England more or less in its original form (though not its original buildings) is that at Winchester, the Hospital of St Cross. It was founded in 1136 by Henry de Blois, Bishop of Winchester and brother of King Stephen, for thirteen poor men 'for the health of my soul and the souls of my predecessors and of the kings of England . . . that the poor in Christ may there humbly and devoutly serve God'.

We have in these brief details some clues to the origin of almshouses in England, which are as varied in their sizes and styles as ordinary dwelling houses, ranging from humble single cottages to spectacular architectural compositions. They occur in our towns and cities and some villages, and are often to be found close to the parish church. Indeed, in a few cases, they were actually built in churchyards, so close were they to the heart of the Church. But they were not, as is often thought, an invention of Christianity.

The modern word 'alms' comes from the Greek *eleēmosunē* (compassion) via the Old English *aelmysse*, and there is plenty of evidence that the ancient world provided care and hospitality for the sick and infirm, not only in classical Europe but also in India and elsewhere, and before Christianity demonstrated its concern for the poor, from not entirely unselfish motives, Islam was taking practical measures to shelter those who needed care. The earliest English almshouses, however, were closely linked with the Church, though not always founded by it. The Council of Nicaea in 325 and the Synod of Aix in 816 both admonished the Church to provide for the poor and the sick, as well as widows and strangers, with a monk or priest to be set in charge of each establishment.

Rotha Mary Clay, in her 1909 book on the medieval hospitals, wrote that 'almshouse', 'hospital' and 'bede-house' were words used indiscriminately to describe the same thing, but this seems to have been so only at a later period, and we can distinguish them a little if we are to start at the beginning and understand the origins of what we now invariably call alms-houses.

Medieval buildings founded by the monasteries for the care and treatment of the sick were called 'infirmaries', and most were originally within the monastic precincts, for the benefit of lay monks and brethren. There were also specialized establishments such as 'lazar houses', for the isolation of leprosy victims, and 'pest-houses', for those suffering from pestilential diseases like the plague, as well as asylums for the insane.

A 'hospital' was not specifically for the treatment of the sick, but for the housing and care of the poor, especially the old. It was a place of hospitality; a charitable establishment for the reception of the infirm, and travellers – especially pilgrims – needing temporary shelter. It was supported by the gifts of money called 'alms', collected by the Church for its maintenance. In France it was often called a *Maison Dieu*, and it is by that name that some of the earliest English almshouses were known. It differed from the later almshouses mainly in having a large common room with a chapel at the end, instead of separate quarters or tenements for each inmate. This 'infirmary hall' was probably at first like a modern hospital ward, with beds along the walls, but later it was divided into cubicles with wooden partitions. In so far as sickness was treated at all in these early establishments, it was treated with antipathetic magic – driving out the evil spirits which the Church believed to possess the sufferer. The name was sometimes abbreviated to 'spital' – hence Spitalfields was the site of a medieval hospital, dedicated to St Mary, which has long since disappeared.

Those almshouses founded by individual benefactors from religious motives were sometimes called bede-houses, and their inmates bedesmen or bedeswomen. 'Bede' means prayer, and bede-houses are distinguished from hospitals and almshouses only by the fact that they were founded specifically so that the poor inside might spend the rest of their lives in grateful prayer for the souls of their benefactors. This act of founder-worship was often required in medieval almshouses and hospitals, too, but it was not necessarily the sole reason for their foundation,

The crypt of St Leonard's Hospital, York

whereas with bede-houses it was the *raison d'être*, and was usually associated with a chantry chapel. The resident priest was thus assured for all time of a captive congregation.

The first English hospitals of which we have any record preceded the Conquest, one being mentioned at St Albans in 794, and another being founded, according to tradition, in the tenth century at York by the Saxon king Athelstan, who granted the site and endowed it with *thraves*, a portion of the corn produced by each of his Northumbrian subjects. It was dedicated to St Peter. There were doubtless many other Saxon hospitals of which we know nothing, but another is mentioned in Yorkshire at Flixton, which was a place of refuge to preserve travellers 'from being devoured by wolves and other voracious forest beasts', according to a charter of Henry VI's time.

The hospital at York was badly damaged by fire in 1137, and was re-founded by King Stephen in 1155 and dedicated to St Leonard. It accommodated 224 inmates by 1370, and had three chapels – an establishment of a size rarely matched in later foundations. Monarchs conferred benefactions on it and it was under the patronage of the canons of York Minster, but it is now in ruins, with only the walls of one of the chapels standing to any height. As an ecclesiastical establishment, it was a victim of the Dissolution in December 1539.

King Athelstan is also associated by tradition with the foundation of hospitals at Bath and Malmesbury, both with the common early dedication to St John, but there is no evidence to support these attributions. At Pontefract, however, a hospital dedicated to St Nicholas was founded soon after the Conquest by the lord of the manor, Robert de Lacy.

Many other hospitals preceded the surviving foundations at Winchester and elsewhere. Around 1084 Archbishop Lanfranc founded St John's Hospital at Canterbury as well as a lazar house at Harbledown, a little to the west of the city. St John's accommodated no less than a hundred poor people of both sexes who, because of their age, or disease, were incapable of earning their bread. They included blind, deaf and lame people. The sexes were segregated, both in the chapel and in the hospital buildings. The huge hall, built of flint with dressings of Caen limestone, was 150 feet long, separated into two halves for men and women, and there was an adjoining small building which is thought to have been a mortuary. The chapel was also divided into two halves. The hospital no doubt profited greatly from the alms of pilgrims to the chief cathedral city of England, and at one period it is said that a proctor sold indulgences for the hospital's benefit, exempting the purchasers from 30,000 Paternosters and Ave Marias. But frauds took advantage of the opportunity to pose as collectors of alms, or as pardoners, and men were occasionally arrested for receiving money and goods 'ostensibly for that house'.

The hospital suffered a disastrous fire in the fourteenth century, and only a part of its chapel survived, but in the present chapel Archbishop Lanfranc's original intention of keeping the men and women separate is still observed. The accommodation for the lepers at Harbledown was only in wooden buildings. Sixty men and women were housed there. The chapel was built of flint, and part of this survives, though largely rebuilt in the seventeenth century. The floor has a distinct slope downward from the altar to the west door, and it has been suggested that this was deliberately designed so that the chapel could be swilled out after the lepers had attended Mass.

St John's Hospital has remained in use and the lazar house, like many others, was also converted into almshouses when leprosy had been virtually eliminated from Britain; but the buildings today bear little resemblance to the originals, St John's having a Tudor half-timbered entrance gate in front of Victorian almshouses, and Harbledown's present buildings being mostly of the nineteenth century.

It is said of the latter that Erasmus of Rotterdam visited it in the company of his friend John Colet, Dean of St Paul's, and that the Dean was so blistering in his refusal to kiss a holy relic presented by one of the inmates, that the gentle Erasmus made amends by putting a generous donation in the almsbox. This is still preserved, with a length of chain by which it was once hung from a tree by the roadside, so that pilgrims and other passers-by could give money without getting too close to the lepers.

Bishop Wulstan founded a hospital near Worcester around 1085, and there was also a hospital for the shelter of pilgrims at Battle by that time. In the twelfth century, when the monasteries had become well established and often wealthy, pilgrims were always on the roads, and many hospitals provided for them, particularly in the Southeast and East Anglia.

At Lewes in Sussex, two hospitals existed in the eleventh century, dedicated to St James and St Nicholas. Both provided for thirteen poor men and women, but St Nicholas's may have been a leper hospital. They were connected with the Cluniac priory in the town, and St James's at least, if not both, was probably founded by the lord of the manor, William de Warenne, who, with his wife Gundruda, also founded the priory, following his visit to Cluny during a pilgrimage to Rome. The hospital stood close to the priory gates, and what remains of it is partly incorporated in the present church of St John Baptist. At the Dissolution, thirteen men and a woman lost the roof over their heads, when the king's agent Thomas Cromwell employed an Italian engineer to demolish the priory's buildings.

Bishop Gundulf founded a hospital at Chatham in the twelfth century, dedicated to St Bartholomew, but little of that building remains, even the flint chapel having been much restored. Nothing at all survives of the original hospital founded in 1123

at Smithfield in London by one Rahere, said to have been at one
time court minstrel to Henry I, who granted him the land for the
hospital he vowed to build if he recovered from an illness he
suffered whilst in Rome. By this time he was an Augustinian
canon. We see here again that the medieval motive for founding
charities was, if sometimes genuine pity for the poor and the
sick, also sometimes from self-interest. Charity was conditional
on doing a mutually beneficial deal with God.

The hospital at Smithfield, also dedicated to St Bartholomew,
accommodated blind and sick persons, and even insane ones, as
well as the poor, and the butchers of Smithfield, among others,
contributed to its upkeep. Bartholomew Fair was inaugurated
by Henry I in 1133 for the hospital's financial benefit, and
survived for over 700 years, being abolished as a nuisance in
1855, by which time it had deteriorated into a pleasure fair
lasting a fortnight.

St Bartholomew's was dissolved and then refounded by Henry
VIII in response to a petition from the Lord Mayor and citizens
of London, but the present Bart's is, of course, a hospital in the
modern medical sense and its buildings date mostly from the
eighteenth century. The tomb of Rahere is in the church of St
Bartholomew the Great, founded by him at the same time as the
hospital, as part of an Augustinian priory.

Bart's did not take in lepers, but some early hospitals were
closely linked with and often modelled on the lazar houses. At
Winchester, for instance, we know that a leper hospital dedicated to St Mary Magdalene had a series of separate cells or
cubicles for the lepers, as well as a master's house and a chapel.
And when Henry de Blois founded the Hospital of St Cross in the
town in 1136, it was based on a similar arrangement.

We know of more than two hundred medieval 'lazar houses'
or leprosy hospitals, which sometimes became almshouses in
later times. For instance, the Empress Maud founded lazar
houses in York and London in the twelfth century. But the
foundations and history of most of these early hospitals are lost
in obscurity, and their buildings long vanished, and we must
confine ourselves to those few which have survived in the later
form as almshouses.

It is probable that the uniform or other means of distinguishing a hospital inmate, from the medieval period onward, was

carried on from the practice in leper colonies, as well as the general building layout. The dread of lepers in the Middle Ages, based partly on the mistaken and still prevalent belief that the disease is highly contagious, and partly on revulsion at the leper's deformities, meant a life sentence for victims. The authorities in charge of lepers in the Middle Ages did not, in fact, subscribe to the belief in the contagiousness of the disease, but the public at large did, in no uncertain terms. Diagnosis was in the hands of priests, who ordered the sufferer's isolation, and his ostracization was completed by the compulsory garment or distinguishing sign by which the unafflicted might be warned of his approach, not to mention the bell or clapperboards he was forced to carry, for lepers were occasionally let out to beg for alms in the streets, but were forbidden to enter market places or narrow lanes, and to touch gates or doors without their gloves on.

Probably about half the hospitals we know of in the early medieval period were founded originally as lazar houses, or hospitals specifically for lepers, although the proportion was higher in some counties, notably Norfolk and Suffolk, suggesting a steady influx of sufferers from across the North Sea. Elsewhere, provision was just as often for the old and infirm without any connotation of disease or infection at all.

Other hospitals founded early in the twelfth century included one at Cirencester for three poor men and three poor women, of which fragments of the original buildings remain; one at Norwich which survived until the Dissolution and then became a prison for 'lazy beggars'; one at Ilford, originally for thirteen lepers; and one at Reading, founded by the abbot of Reading Abbey for twenty-six poor people as well as providing hospitality for strangers and pilgrims.

The hospital at Ilford was founded by an abbess of Barking Abbey, Adelicia, and dedicated to St Mary the Blessed Virgin. About thirty years after its foundation, the chapel was reconsecrated by another abbess, Mary, who was Thomas Becket's sister, and she added her brother's name to the dedication. It was recognized after the Dissolution as an almshouse for six poor men, having been granted by Queen Elizabeth to Thomas Fanshaw on the understanding that this was to be done, and the hospital still exists, though the buildings apart from the chapel are all modern.

Remains of St John's Hospital, Cirencester

There is an interesting record, quoted by R. M. Clay from an eighteenth-century book of *Curious Discourses*, of the expulsion of a leper from this hospital for improper behaviour. He had, it seems, 'brought into his chamber a drab, and sayd she was his sister'. He was made to do penance in the chapel, kneeling on the altar steps, bareheaded and with bare feet, throughout Mass, and then the priest 'disgraded him of orders, scraped his hands and his crown with a knife, took his booke from him, gave him a boxe on the chiek with the end of his fingers, and then thrust him out of the churche, where the officers and people receyved him, and putt him into a carte, cryinge, *Ha rou, Ha rou, Ha rou*, after him.'

More or less contemporary with the Hospital of St Cross at Winchester was St Giles's at Wilton in Wiltshire, founded as a lazar house, according to tradition, by Adelaide of Louvain, second wife of Henry I. According to an inscription once to be seen on the chapel door, the queen was herself a leper, and had 'window and dore from her lodgeing into the chancell of the chapel, whence she heard prayer. She lieth buried under a marble gravestone'. This legend, however, dates from the rebuilding of the hospital in 1624, the establishment having survived the Dissolution on account of its supposed royal connection. In fact, Adelaide married again after Henry's death, and died in Flanders. Perhaps it was a close relative of hers who was a leper, and she founded the hospital on that account. At any rate, only a small part of the original chapel remains, though the foundation itself survives in a reduced form. We know that Richard II installed one of his aged servants there in about 1385.

Henry I himself founded St Bartholomew's at Cowley, Oxford, partly as a lazar house, and it remains, now in the hands of Oriel College, but none of the original buildings or chapel survive, the present chapel dating from the fourteenth century when Edward III made over the establishment to the college founded by his father.

Uniform of the brothers of the de Blois foundation at Winchester – black cap and gown with silver cross

Although little remains of the original buildings of St Cross
except the church and sacristy, this great hospital at Winchester
is the oldest such establishment which survives, in essence, as its
founder intended it to be, eight and a half centuries ago. We can
therefore use it as a basis for comparison with all later almshouses. It was to accommodate thirteen poor men, a number
common in charitable establishments, and having no conno-
tations of ill-luck in those days, the sum of Christ and his
apostles being thought a holy number rather than as a portent
based on the Last Supper.

St Cross developed as a community on the south side of the
city, and its parish church was founded and built by Henry de
Blois at the same time as the hospital which adjoined it. The
cruciform church took over a century to complete, and is a
mixture of Romanesque and Gothic styles, with much early use
of Purbeck 'marble'.

The foundation came at a time when there was a great and
urgent need for charity. It was a critical period in English history,
when even men who had been wealthy and powerful were forced
to beg alms in the streets. The *Anglo-Saxon Chronicle* records of
1137, the year after St Cross was founded: 'Then was corn dear
and flesh and cheese and butter, for none there was in the land.
The wretched people perished with hunger; some, who had been
great men, were driven to beggary, while others fled from the
country . . . and men said openly that Christ and His saints
slept.'

During the first half of the church's building period, the
hospital itself underwent several changes of management.
Bishop de Blois himself passed its administration over to the
Knights of St John of Jerusalem the year after he founded it, but
there seems to have been much dispute about their rights to its
control. They surrendered it to the Bishop of Winchester in
1185, but the Pope gave it back to them two years later, and their
rightful possession was afterwards confirmed by Richard I,
though they again lost and regained it in the reign of King John,
finally submitting to the then bishop's claim in 1200, since when
the appointment of the Master has always been made by the
bishops of Winchester.

Henry de Blois also provided for a hundred poor men 'of good
character' to be given a meal at the hospital every day, and this

medieval tradition survives in a watered-down version (if one may use the expression) in the provision of a 'wayfarer's dole' of ale and a morsel of bread, given to any caller who asks for it. The cups and serving boards, like the dark gowns of the pensioners, bear the Greek cross – the symbol of the hospital's original trustees, the Knights Hospitallers – which also appears on the buildings. This dispensation to outsiders was not, at the time, peculiar to Winchester. St Leonard's, York, and St Giles's, Norwich, were among other hospitals where food and drink were provided for callers. But St Cross is the only one where a vestige of the medieval tradition has been preserved.

The so-called 'Hundred Men's Hall' where the meal was served in medieval times was on the east side of the entrance court. The Brethren's Hall – the common hall for the hospital's inmates – had a central square hearth for a charcoal fire in the winter months, as well as a minstrels' gallery, and was built over a vaulted cellar or undercroft. It has now gone, but much of the establishment refounded and rebuilt in 1446 by Cardinal Beaufort survives in something like its original form. Cardinal Beaufort extended the foundation with what he called the 'Almshouses of Noble Poverty', but some additional dwellings he built were demolished in the eighteenth century. His foundation survives, however, and its pensioners are distinguished from those of the earlier foundation by a different costume, theirs being of a mulberry colour instead of black, and their hats having tassels.

The dwellings form one long range on the west side of the main courtyard, now a lawn with a sundial at the centre, and usually referred to as the 'quadrangle' though it is not square and has more than four sides. The dwellings are very much like the monks' cells in Carthusian monasteries, each pensioner having his own entrance passage, sitting room, bedroom, scullery and lavatory, the latter built like medieval manor house *garde-robes*, projecting out at the back to drain into a watercourse, with the brethren's kitchen garden behind. The quadrangle is entered via the Beaufort Tower, a massive gatehouse with a kneeling figure of the cardinal in a niche. Another niche probably contained an effigy of Bishop de Blois. The Beaufort arms are in the spandrels of the entrance arch, above which a moulded cornice has heads believed to represent Henry IV, his father John of Gaunt, and

The dwellings at St Cross, Winchester

Katherine Swynford, Gaunt's third wife and Cardinal Beaufort's mother, among others.

Between this tower and the pensioners' dwellings is the former master's house, and along this north side and the west range of the quadrangle are tall octagonal chimney stacks in military formation. Opposite the west range is an ambulatory or cloister, above which was formerly the infirmary, this part dating from the sixteenth century.

This magnificent ancient foundation not only set a standard by which all subsequent almshouses might be judged, but is also testimony to the priorities of the bishop and the cardinal whose names are associated with it; and we shall find similar considerations in connection with many of the medieval almshouses we look at. First, the wealth of the founder was expended primarily on the church or chapel which accompanied all almshouses, and which all inmates were required to attend regularly as a condition of their admittance. Second, the founder believed himself to be providing for the good of his own soul by his act of charity, earning – if not indeed compelling – the prayers of the inmates for their benefactor; for as Thomas Aquinas was to express it, withholding alms when there is evident and urgent necessity is mortal sin. Nietzsche wrote: 'If all alms were given only from pity, all beggars would have starved long ago'. This may be a cynical exaggeration, but it is undoubtedly true that many medieval almshouses founded by monarchs and churchmen originated in self-interest, the welfare of the poor being merely incidental. Bishop de Blois, for instance, was no saint. He was a warmongering and ambitious Norman baron who had encouraged Stephen to seize the throne of England, and was put out when his brother did not make him Archbishop of Canterbury. And Bishop Ranulph of Durham, who founded a hospital for thirteen poor men, was 'the most infamous prince of publicans', widely execrated in his day. He was adviser to William Rufus, and enriched himself and the king without scruple.

St Mary Magdalene's Hospital at King's Lynn dates from 1145, when a prior and twelve people of either sex were accommodated, of whom nine were to be 'sound' and three leprous. It seems to have avoided dissolution, though much reduced, and was refounded by James I. And St Albans had a leper hospital founded by Abbot Geoffrey de Gorham in 1146, subject to the abbey's rule and dedicated to St Julian. It was run with strict discipline. Part of the inmates' compulsory dress was high boots, and if one was discovered wearing low shoes 'tied with only one knot', he was made to walk barefoot for a season.

In 1148 Matilda of Boulogne, King Stephen's queen, founded the hospital of St Katharine-by-the-Tower in London. This was a very large establishment, and the fact that it was of royal rather than ecclesiastical foundation saved it from dissolution by Henry VIII. Several monarchs or their consorts had further endowed it, Henry III's queen, Eleanor of Provence, in particular, having refounded it in 1273 for ten poor women and six scholar-boys and various staff, and reserving its patronage for the queens of England. The inmates were to pray for the souls of the foundress and her ancestors, as the original inmates more than a century before were intended to pray for the souls of Matilda's children. The hospital survived until 1825, when it was demolished to make way for the building of St Katharine's Dock. The restored chapel still stands, now the church of London's Danish community, and the hospital foundation survives as the St Katharine Royal Foundation at Stepney, carrying out social work in London's east end.

An ecclesiastical foundation of around 1160 at Coventry,

intended as a house of 'perpetual pity' for poor and infirm of both sexes, was a victim of the Dissolution, being replaced by a grammar school. But a hospital of about the same time, or possibly earlier, at Northampton, founded for eight poor men by an archdeacon of Peterborough, became extinct through misappropriation of its funds by successive masters – a not infrequent cause of demise in charitable establishments, as we shall see. The chapel eventually became a Roman Catholic church, the common infirmary hall a caretaker's house, and the master's house was later demolished to make way for the railway station.

At Stamford, Lincolnshire, a hospital dedicated to St John the Baptist and St Thomas the Martyr was founded around 1174 by one Brand de Fossato who, according to a letter from his bishop, 'guided by divine inspiration, having sold all you possess, have erected a certain hospital and chapel . . . where you have chose to exhibit a perpetual offering to your creator'. This foundation was under the patronage of the abbey at Peterborough, and it became a victim of dissolution.

At Peterborough an abbot founded St Thomas's 'to the honour of his old master', who now began to be accounted a saint and a martyr. The abbot, Benedict, had been Becket's chancellor at Canterbury. The Peterborough establishment naturally disappeared in the Tudor period, although two others founded at about the same time – 1180 – in Bath and High Wycombe, survive to this day. Both were dedicated to St John the Baptist and the one at Bath, at least, was of ecclesiastical origin. It was spared, perhaps, because it was intended for those who came seeking the benefit of the mineral springs. The founder of the High Wycombe hospital is unknown, but it was doubtless a churchman, for it was refounded by Elizabeth I, and must therefore have been much reduced, if not altogether suppressed. The original buildings are in ruins, but their walls contain material from a former Roman villa nearby.

Meanwhile, the Church's English capital, Canterbury, quite properly held itself up to the nation as an example of the charitable works expected of Christians everywhere. Around 1175 a hospital, dedicated to the recently murdered and even more recently canonized St Thomas à Becket, was founded at Eastbridge 'for the maintenance of poor pilgrims and other infirm persons resorting thither to remain until they are healed of their infirmities'. Some liked to think it was founded by Becket himself, but this does not seem to be so. The common hall was built of flint with a groin-vaulted undercroft, and Romanesque wall paintings remain in it, including a scene of Becket's martyrdom and a seated figure of Christ, which Graham Sutherland may have seen and recalled when designing his tapestry 'Christ in Majesty' for the new Coventry Cathedral. The chapel was on the upper floor, across one end of the hall at right angles to it.

The twelfth-century seal of the Hospital of Holy Innocents at Lincoln, showing a leper begging for alms

Much rebuilding was done here in the fourteenth century, by which time Archbishop Stratford had placed increased emphasis on hospitality for pilgrims – 'for persons going to Rome, for others coming to Canterbury and needing shelter, and for lying-in women'. In the sixteenth century Leland could still refer to it as 'An Hospital within the Town on the Kinges Bridge for poore Pylgrems and way faring men', and Archbishop Whitgift later turned it into a school for twenty boys, but it subsequently reverted to its original purpose, and remains an almshouse today, with the almsmen and women living in half-timbered cottages behind the old infirmary hall. A poor priests' hospital and one for leprous monks had been added to Canterbury's charitable foundations by early in the thirteenth century, both now gone.

At the northern end of England, meanwhile, the hospital at Sherburn near Durham was founded in 1181 by the bishop,

Hugh Pudsey, as a hospital for sixty-five lepers of either sex.
They were divided into five convents of thirteen each, and they
all had to attend Mass daily. Severe discipline was maintained in
this establishment, even to the extent of corporal punishment.
For disobedience or bad behaviour, inmates were caned like
schoolboys, and during Lent they were beaten in a purification
ritual – a rare instance of flagellation in England. They were well
fed, however – meat, fish and poultry were regular parts of their
diet, as well as dairy produce, fruit and vegetables, and on festive
occasions they might even have fresh salmon or goose. Fuel was
provided for their winter fires and woollen cloth for their
garments, and an annual dole was established on the anniversary
of the death of one of the first masters.

At St Leonard's, Lancaster, founded for lepers in 1189 by the
prince soon to become King John, the master was himself a leper,
and at Chatham and Ilford, too, provision was made for one of
the leprous inmates to be appointed master.

Early in the fifteenth century, some misappropriation of the
Sherburn hospital's funds was taking place, and the Pope issued
a new constitution in 1434 establishing a clerk in holy orders as
its master, subject only to the authority of the bishop. By this
time, leprosy had so far declined in England that only two places
were reserved for lepers here, and the hospital became what we
would now call an almshouse, surviving the Dissolution,
surprisingly, despite its ecclesiastical origins. Little of the original hospital remains today, the buildings having been subject to
much rebuilding after damage by fire and Scots raiders. But the
charity remains in operation on its original site, the present
buildings being mainly Victorian Gothic.

Less fortunate were the hospitals of St Saviour at Bury St
Edmunds, founded in 1184, and St Mary Spital at London's
Bishopsgate, founded in 1197. The Suffolk establishment was
founded by the abbot and convent for twelve men and twelve
women at first, but it seems that eventually the women were
thrown out to make way for elderly and infirm clergymen. It was
a place of some importance, evidently, for just before the Wars
of the Roses, Henry VI held a parliament there, and ordered the
arrest of his uncle Humphrey, Duke of Gloucester, whom he
accused of planning an uprising. Legend has it that Humphrey
was murdered there. It is hardly surprising, all the same, that a

place of such holy emphasis should fall victim to dissolution, and the same fate befell the Bishopsgate hospital which was founded specifically for Augustinian brethren.

Tales of miracle cures had become attached to several hospitals in those blindly religious times; even lazar houses, as at Darlington, for instance, where a young woman at the late-twelfth-century Bathele Spital who was 'grievously tormented with a loathsome leprosy' was miraculously healed by St Godric who 'removed the noxious humours'. We are entitled to doubt both the authenticity of the miracles and the diagnosis of the disease, since it seems likely that many suffering from other deformities and skin diseases – eczema for instance – were called lepers.

It was put down to miraculous recovery that a woman who had been hanged at Lincoln for harbouring a thief (her son) was found to be alive just before she was buried, and Margaret Everard was thus pardoned and permitted to live at Holy Innocents Hospital, which was founded as a lazar house by Henry I.

The Hospital of St John the Baptist at Lutterworth in Leicestershire was probably founded in order to secure a place in paradise for Rosia de Verdon and her son Nicholas, as was St Julian's at Southampton, founded by two brothers who were wealthy merchants of the town. This hospital was known also as God's House, and its modern buildings adjoin the restored chapel which is now known as the 'French church' on account of its use by French-speaking Protestants since the sixteenth century. Three traitors executed by Henry V were buried in this chapel – the king's cousin Richard Plantagenet; Henry, Lord Scrope, and Sir Thomas Grey. Queen's College, Oxford, was granted custody of this hospital in 1343, and the modern almshouses remain under the college's protection.

King John had good cause for concern about the state of his conscience, and he may have founded the Hospital of St Bartholomew at Newbury, granting it a fair on the saint's day. The present buildings on the south side of the town date only from the seventeenth century, and the chapel long ago became a school, but survival of the Dissolution and a charter of Elizabeth I vesting the hospital in the town's corporation suggest royal foundation.

King John is thought to have founded a leper hospital at Bristol, as well as the one at Lancaster already noticed, while he was yet a prince, and John Bale's sixteenth-century play *King John* refers to him thus:

Never prynce was there that made to poore peoples use
So many masendewes, hospytals and spyttle howses,
As your grace hath done yet sens the worlde began.

St John's at Oxford enjoyed royal patronage from its foundation in King John's reign until the fifteenth century when all the foundation's estates were granted by Henry VI to William Waynflete, Bishop of Winchester, who founded Magdalen College on the extensive site beside the River Cherwell. Only fragments of the hospital are now traceable.

In 1213 came St Thomas's in Southwark, which survived and grew to become, like Bart's, one of the great modern medical hospitals, though not now on its original site like its fellow hospital over the river. St Thomas's was built by the Prior of Bermondsey to accommodate converts from Judaism and poor children, and was attached to the Priory of St Mary Overie. Although it was suppressed by Henry VIII in spite of a petition from local citizens, Edward VI reversed the decision and refounded it as an infirmary, granting it to the mayor and citizens.

Nothing remains at Bridgwater, Somerset, of the hospital dedicated to St John the Baptist which stood here in King John's time, but a house of like dedication at Wilton in the first years of his successor, intended for two men and two women, is still a going concern, notwithstanding its probable ecclesiastical origin. Almshouses were built in place of the old hospital buildings, and even parts of the former chapel were converted into dwellings.

The medieval hospitals often had their own official seals, unless they were of monastic origin, when the seal of the order was common to them, too. In cases where the hospital was founded for lepers, the seal would often show a leper on crutches, or being attended by a monk. In other establishments, the seals might show the buildings, or images of their founders, or of Christ, or of the saints to whom they were dedicated. Seals

Medieval remains of St John's Hospital, Malmesbury

were usually of oval or lozenge shape, and some were very impressive.

Few, if any, medieval houses of pity have achieved more fame than Harnham Hospital at Salisbury, more properly called St Nicholas's. It was founded in 1220 by Richard Poore, Bishop of Salisbury, for eight poor men and four poor women, and it owes its fame to being popularly regarded as the model for 'Hiram's Hospital' in the first of Anthony Trollope's 'Barsetshire' novels, *The Warden* and *Barchester Towers*. In truth, there are better grounds for regarding St Cross at Winchester as Trollope's model, as we shall see. At Salisbury, at any rate, the real hospital takes its name from Harnham Bridge over the River Avon, close to which it stands, south of the cathedral close, and if its story is not quite as dramatic as the fictional version, nor its personalities so colourful as the worldly Dr Grantly, the hypocritical Slope and the unspeakable Mrs Proudie, at least its genuine history and its survival place it in the front rank of medieval almshouses.

To begin with, the hall and chapel were divided into two halves, no doubt for segregation of the sexes, like Archbishop Lanfranc's foundation of more than a century earlier at Canterbury. The common hall also seems to have been aisled, like the nave of a church or a Norman lord's great hall, perhaps into what we would now call a men's and a women's ward. A further point of interest is that we know that the hospital managed to avoid suppression at the Dissolution by devious means, with the connivance of the earls of Pembroke at nearby Wilton, who concealed from the king's visitors the religious connections of the hospital. It was restored and reconstituted by James I in 1610, and although only fragments of the medieval buildings remain, the foundation is still thriving, its modern almshouses on the site being mainly Victorian.

In the year after the foundation of Harnham, Dover saw the erection of its Maison Dieu, endowed by Hubert de Burgh for poor people and the hospitality of pilgrims, and dedicated to St Mary. This also seems to have had a divided infirmary hall, rather longer than Salisbury's. The Plantagenet and Lancastrian kings exercised their right to lodge there on their journeys to France, but as with certain other hospitals which had to put up with rich patrons and their retinues expecting hospitality, this use was considered by many an unwarranted burden, and a

*The ancient foundation known as Harnham Hospital, Salisbury
is now housed in modern buildings*

deprivation of the poor. Despite the royal interest in it and the
welcome endowments this brought, the Dover hospital was
dissolved in 1544, and the Admiralty was granted the site as a
victualling yard, but in 1834 the town acquired it, and the
surviving part of the medieval hall is now the eastern half of the
town hall, looking like a church with its traceried Gothic

windows and flint walls with ragstone dressings. The restored chapel building became the magistrates' court.

At Sandwich, however, St Bartholomew's, founded at about the same time, is still going, because its origins were more secular than religious. It was apparently endowed from the spoils of a battle at sea, and a Lord Warden of the Cinque Ports, whose tomb is in the chapel, was possibly the founder, and certainly one of the hospital's benefactors. The place was intended for 'Maryners desesid and hurt' according to Leland. Nineteenth-century cottages house the present pensioners, but the fine original thirteenth-century chapel remains.

The year 1229 saw the foundation of another fine medieval hospital which happily survives – St Mary's at Chichester. This was originally a convent, dating from 1172, but Henry III reconstituted it for the housing of thirteen poor men and the hospitality of pilgrims and the sick, and surviving documents give us some fascinating insights into medieval priorities in caring for those in need. 'In regard to the poor who are received late at night and go forth in the morning', for example, 'let the Warden take care that their feet are washed'.

St Mary's is unique among English almshouses in being the only remaining example of a medieval hospital layout where separate dwellings are contained within the common hall. It is a huge surprise to enter the hall, looking very much like a church, and find tiny houses built inside, as in the aisles of a nave. These dwellings date from the seventeenth century, each one having its own bedroom, kitchen and sitting room, and more recently, its own bathroom as well. But the main structure of the building, its lofty roof supported on huge timbers with later brick chimney stacks rising through them, dates from the late thirteenth century, when Edward I confirmed the establishment under the administration of the Dean and Chapter of Chichester Cathedral, and the original hospital was largely rebuilt. The chapel is separated from the hall only by a splendid Decorated oak screen, so that the medieval inmates who could not walk to the chapel could hear the services from their beds.

The establishment was somewhat reduced at the Dissolution, only five inmates being accommodated in the reign of Elizabeth I, but then three more were added later, and all eight of them – the current number – were women. The present old ladies enjoy modern housing standards and central heating, but their medieval predecessors were subject to more rigorous conditions and stern discipline: 'if a brother shall have a quarrel with a brother with noise and riot, then let him fast for seven days, on Wednesdays and Fridays, on bread and water, and sit at the bottom of the table and without a napkin'. Moreover, the warden was enjoined to examine very carefully the status and character of anyone who applied for admission, and to point out to him 'the poverty of the House, the poorness of the food, the gravity of the obedience, and the heavy duties, which may possibly deter him and induce him to recall his purpose'.

The present inhabitants are still required to be of good character, able to look after themselves, and must attend a service in the chapel every day. The Dean is in fact very strict with these old ladies, who are in their eighties or nineties, insisting that they must be in by ten o'clock at night! But their accommodation is free, only their food and clothing being their own responsibility, and they have very peaceful and well-tended gardens to enjoy in the warmer weather.

At Exeter, the hospital of St John the Baptist was founded in 1230. The reader will not have failed to notice what a large proportion of the medieval almshouses we have considered so far are in cathedral cities, but St John's was not of ecclesiastical origin, being founded by two brothers, John and Gilbert Long. Soon afterwards an older hospital dedicated to St Alexius, and also founded by a citizen of Exeter, was incorporated with it, and John Long became its master, but it eventually passed to the bishops of Exeter, and was surrendered to the king in 1534.

The lord of the manor of Kingston Lacy in Dorset is said to have founded St Margaret's Hospital at Pamphill, near Wimborne Minster, around 1241, and it may have been a lazar house at first. An old tradition ascribes it to John of Gaunt, but this seems unlikely, as it was never a wealthy foundation, and in any case, it seems that Pope Innocent IV granted indulgences, long before Gaunt's time, to local citizens who supported the hospital with money, absolving them of 'offences done against fader and moder, and all swerynges neglygently made'. The indulgence was to 'hold good for 51 years and 260 days', provided they repeated a certain specified number of Paternosters and Ave Marias daily. The foundation and the chapel are extant, the pensioners now living in separate single-storey dwellings which were built to accommodate three single men, three single women, and three married couples.

St Mary's Hospital at Glastonbury was founded about 1246, possibly on the site of an earlier such establishment, and the chapel of that date survives, with its twin bellcote. On the gable of the chapel one can see the roof line of the former infirmary hall to which the chapel was joined, but two rows of later almshouses now stand detached from it on the ground occupied by the original hall.

St Edmund's at Gateshead and St Giles's at Norwich were founded within two years of each other, but nothing remains of the former except the chapel which became the south aisle of Holy Trinity Church, while the latter survives, having undergone various changes of name and character. It is now generally known, not without reason, as the Great Hospital. Founded by Walter de Suffield, Bishop of Norwich, in 1249, the original organization of this medieval hospital, close to the cathedral, is slightly puzzling. The dedication to St Giles, patron saint of lepers, beggars and cripples, suggests a leper hospital, but there seems to be no evidence that it ever was that, and Bishop de Suffield intended it for 'decrepit chaplains', providing also for thirteen poor men to be given one meal a day. There was certainly the usual common hall with chapel at the end, but at some stage a central part of the long building was rebuilt as the parish church of St Helen, with the remaining part of the infirmary hall on one side and the chaplains' chapel on the other. (Later still, the chapel itself was converted into wards on two floors.) Meanwhile, the whole complex had taken on the appearance of a monastery, with dining hall, master's house and dormitories ranged round a cloister on the north side of the hall and church. It accommodated eight Augustinian chaplains, seven scholars, four sisters and eight bed-ridden poor folk. How on earth did this place evade dissolution? Only, it seems, by being spared temporarily by Henry VIII as a result of a petition from the citizens of Norwich, and then being suppressed as an ecclesiastical establishment by Edward VI who granted it to the corporation instead, since when it has carried on its good work, with nineteenth-century almshouses now grouped round the surviving medieval buildings. The ceiling of the former chapel is

St Mary's Hospital, Chichester – the unique medieval hall

one of the most fortunate preservations, being decorated with
252 heraldic spread eagles, said to be in honour of Anne of
Bohemia, Richard II's queen, who visited the hospital at the time
of its reconstruction.

At Maidstone, in 1260, Archbishop Boniface founded a hospital for travellers, especially poor pilgrims on their way to
Canterbury. It was known as the Newark hospital or Boniface's,
but was dedicated to St Peter and St Paul. But in 1395 it was
combined by Archbishop Courtenay with a college for priests,
and thus fell foul of Henry VIII. Some of its buildings are still
standing, though now used for other purposes. They include a
massive battlemented gatehouse with Gothic archway, built of
the hard Kentish ragstone. The original chapel was made into
the parish church of St Peter in the nineteenth century.

A charitable foundation at Stratford-on-Avon is dated 1269,
though the founder is not known. It was of secular origin,
although authorized by the Bishop of Worcester, and connected
with the Guild of the Holy Cross. Sir Hugh Clopton rebuilt the
chapel in the late fifteenth century, and the almshouses, now
forming an attractive street frontage of half-timbered buildings
with overhanging upper storeys and tall brick chimneys, have
also been much altered over the centuries. Between the houses
and the chapel, the guild's original hall became the town hall at
one stage, and then the grammar school where William
Shakespeare was almost certainly educated, being in his place by
the time the chapel bell was rung at six o'clock in the morning.
The chapel itself survived misuse by a vicar who allowed dogs,
pigs and poultry to run free in it, as well as letting his children
play ball and his servants hang clothes to dry there.

At Scarborough, a hospital dedicated to St Nicholas was said
to have been founded by burgesses of the town in the reign of
Edward I. In 1342 the master and brethren were requested to
admit a chaplain, John de Burgh, who had been 'suddenly
attacked by the disease of leprosy, and has not wherewith to live
and is unable through shame to beg among Christians'.

A hospital dedicated to St Laurence was founded as a leper
house at Cirencester in the thirteenth century by Edith Bisset, the
Lady of Wiggold, under the patronage of the abbey, and then
became an almshouse for two poor widows. The foundation is
still in existence, and has grown considerably in modern times.

A little crop of hospitals built in the last twenty years of the thirteenth century deserves notice, these being at Bedford, Newport Pagnell and Tavistock. Bedford saw the foundation of two hospitals at this time, one of them being a lazar house. St John's was intended strictly for decayed freemen of the town, and had a rule that poor folk dwelling outside the town were to be 'expulsed and put out'. It did not long fulfil its obligation, however. The chapel and fragments of the hall are still standing, the latter having been used as a rectory at one time when the hospital had fallen into decay, and the chapel became one of the town's churches.

At Newport Pagnell in Buckinghamshire, a hospital dedicated to St John the Evangelist and St John the Baptist was raised in 1281. It was refounded for three poor men and three poor women by Anne of Denmark, James I's queen, and survives as Queen Anne's Hospital, though all the old buildings have gone.

The Hospital of St Nicholas at Tavistock was in existence by 1286, and according to John Leland, was founded by two of the town's merchants, named Akebarrow and Overstal. Nothing remains, but the foundation survives to remind us that purely religious motivation was not behind all the hundreds of hospitals founded in the Middle Ages, and much less so in the case of those built later, though securing a place in paradise was uppermost in the mind of many an individual benefactor for several centuries. But a social conscience was also in process of development regarding the poor and infirm. In particular, the medieval trade guilds began to provide for members whose useful working lives were at an end, and other hospitals were subject to municipal rather than ecclesiastical administration.

At York, where there were several medieval hospitals, that of St Mary the Greater was founded in 1314 by the Dean, Robert Pykering, but became a school at the Dissolution; but at Rochester, St Catherine's, founded two years later by Symond Potyn for lepers or other sick men, is still in existence, though the medieval buildings have again gone. In Lincoln, the 'Spital on the Street' was founded before 1323, and in Hythe, St Bartholomew's, which still exists, was founded as St Andrew's in Edward III's reign for ten poor people of either sex.

In the far north of England, hospitals were as like as other buildings to be victims of border raids. A God's House at

Berwick-on-Tweed, founded by Philip de Ryedale in 1286, was severely damaged during a siege, and the poor residents were unable to repair the buildings before the winter set in, suffering much hardship as a consequence. Sherburn Hospital at Durham suffered much damage during the Battle of Neville's Cross, in 1346.

At Carlisle, St Nicholas's Hospital, founded by the king (?John) around the beginning of the thirteenth century, was more than once razed to the ground during skirmishes with the red-haired Caledonian battalions from the north, and mismanagement by its masters also contributed to this hospital's troubles. It continued as a leper hospital 'until by lapse of time the greater part of the lepers died, when . . . their places were filled by poor impotent folk'. Not for very long, however. The place eventually disappeared without trace.

In London, meanwhile, a hostel founded in the thirteenth century at Bishopsgate for foreign ecclesiastical visitors had become a hospital, dedicated to St Mary of the Star of Bethlehem, by about 1330. It stood where Liverpool Street Station is now. We do not know whether it was intended exclusively for lunatics at first, or even if they were admitted at all, but they were being taken in by the beginning of the following century, and the hospital was soon specializing in the care (if one can call it that) of the insane. The hospital was not suppressed at the Dissolution, but was given to the City of London, and a new hospital was eventually built at Moorfields, then moved to Lambeth, and in this century to Croydon, where the modern mental hospital known as the Bethlem Royal Hospital is a lot different from the establishment known as 'Bedlam' in Hogarth's time.

Another large hospital grew from its fourteenth-century beginnings at Leicester. Founded in 1330 by the blind Henry of Grosmont, Earl of Lancaster and Leicester, the Newarke College, as it came to be called (from the earl's 'new work') accommodated a hundred poor of both sexes some time later. This establishment owed its name to the fact that the Duke of Lancaster, the earl's son, added to the original foundation a collegiate church, with a dean, canons, vicars, clerks, choristers and nurses. The infirmary hall was 220 feet in length – longer than the naves of some cathedrals – and the foundation was further endowed by John of Gaunt. It stood within a wall which

The chapel of St Mary's, Chichester

enclosed four acres of ground, close to the castle and the River
Soar. Strict rules governed the lives of chaplains and inmates.
Chaplains were not to walk through the town's market place at
night, or to talk to women anywhere.

The church was a fine building in which the first Duke of Lancaster and John of Gaunt's second wife were buried, but it was demolished after the Dissolution, and several splendid marble monuments disappeared with it. The hospital, however, was allowed to remain, and was reconstituted in the seventeenth century as Trinity Hospital. Its master is to this day appointed by the Chancellor of the Duchy of Lancaster, but its present buildings are modern, and all that remains of the medieval college is the so-called Magazine Gateway, a massive stone structure so named after its later use as an armoury. The hospital preserves a huge bronze cauldron, capable of holding more than sixty gallons, which is known as the 'Duke of Lancaster's Porridge Pot'.

During the course of this hospital's development by three Lancastrian earls of Leicester, the Black Death struck Europe, and Henry, Duke of Lancaster, founder of the collegiate church, was one of the plague's victims in the aftermath, Edward III and the Black Prince being among the mourners when he was buried in his own church, not then completed.

The last hospitals built before the Black Death devastated Britain were a leper hospital founded by Ann Boteler at Taddiport in Devon in 1344, of which the chapel survives; a Maison Dieu at Hull, founded by John Kingeston in 1345; followed by another in the same town, for thirteen poor of each sex, founded by Sir William de la Pole, whose family is mentioned in chapter two. This foundation evaded dissolution and survives as the Charterhouse, in brick buildings of the eighteenth century. St Clement's Hospital at Oxford was founded in the same year. After them, winds of change blew through the land.

2 The Black Death and a Century of Changes

The century of the Lancastrian and Yorkist kings of England saw some significant changes in the social structure of the country. The major cause was the Black Death in 1348–9, which probably reduced the country's population by 1½ million people – around a third of the total at that time – and accelerated the new status enjoyed by the country's peasants and labourers.

The immediate effect on treatment of the poor and infirm is at once apparent, in the sudden cessation of new charitable foundations, although in the longer term the foundation of hospitals and bede-houses carried on in much the same way and with similar frequency after the scourge of the Black Death as before it. But there were after-effects. Labour was suddenly scarce, and the former feudal peasants were worth something more than just bodies at the disposal of the manorial lords. The Black Death brought about the free movement of labour and afforded some degree of protection against ruthless exploitation. At the same time, a good deal of arable land was turned to pasture because sheep rearing did not call for such a large labour force as crop growing, and there was less demand for the crops, anyway. Whole villages were wiped out, if not by the plague itself, then by landowners who no longer needed the peasants, but wanted the land the peasants' hovels stood on. Large numbers of rural homeless and unemployed moved to the towns to seek work, and the problem of the urban poor began to assume ominous proportions.

With the Ordinance of Labourers of 1349 and the Statute of Labourers of two years later, the government attempted to check inflation and maintain pre-plague conditions by various economic measures, one of which was to make it illegal to give alms to the able-bodied unemployed. The catastrophic effects on the lives of the poor who survived the epidemics cannot have left

*The so-called 'Long Alley' Almshouses of Christ's Hospital,
Abingdon*

the more humanitarian among the wealthy unmoved, but at the
same time building work was severely curtailed because there
were no longer the numbers of skilled masons and carpenters to
carry it out. Present-day historians constantly warn us against
the danger of over-dramatizing the effects of the Black Death,
but to regard the fairly sudden disappearance of a third of the
nation's adult population as anything less than devastating is
absurd, and as in any national calamity, the poor suffered most.

The period brought not only much poverty but also corruption and mismanagement, so that some of the earlier foundations perished. Lazar houses that could have been put to good
use, no longer having more than the odd leper (for the Black

Death probably reduced leprosy drastically, preying as it did on those least able to resist disease) were allowed to fall down instead. William Langland, the fourteenth-century scourge of the corrupt Church, noted in *Piers the Ploughman* that: 'At one time, Charity consorted with great prelates, with Bishops and Archbishops, and shared out Christ's patrimony among the poor. But nowadays Avarice keeps the keys, reserving all the treasure for his kinsmen'. Langland exhorted the wealthy merchants to use their profits to repair the hospitals ('meson-dieux') and to help folk in trouble.

The Church continued to lay stress on the efficacy of good works, but the Church's influence on common men was diminished by the Black Death, partly because of the high death rate among the clergy who did their Christian duty towards the sick, and partly because people began to question the dogmas of a Church which God appeared to have punished as severely as ordinary men, if not more so. Besides which, the wealth of the Church was under some threat from the political situation, since Parliament needed to raise huge sums of money to finance the king's wars with France.

When Parliament met in the hall of the Grey Friars at Leicester in 1414, proposals for the reformation of hospitals were considered, some from the new young king's erstwhile friend Sir John Oldcastle. The Statute recognized that many of the hospitals were in a sad state. They were said to be 'now for the most part decayed, and the goods and profits of the same, by divers persons, spiritual and temporal, withdrawn and spent to the use of others, whereby many men and women have died in great misery for default of aid, livelihood and succour'. It acknowledged frankly enough that hospitals were founded by 'the noble kings of this realm and lords and ladies both spiritual and temporal as by others of divers estates, in aid and merit of the souls of the said founders'. But it was desired that provisions should be made in 'cities, boroughs and divers other places' for the blind, women in childbirth, those who had lost their property and fallen on hard times, and those who had lost their wits and memory. The will was there, but the money was not. Shakespeare has the Archbishop of Canterbury bemoaning the State's threat, at the beginning of *Henry V*, to deprive the Church of:

As much as would maintain, to the king's honour,
Full fifteen earls and fifteen hundred knights,
Six thousand and two hundred good esquires;
And, to relief of lazars and weak age,
Of indigent faint souls past corporal toil,
A hundred almshouses right well supplied.

The shortage of clergymen also led to abuses of masterships. The Bishop of Winchester's eighteen-year-old nephew was warden of both St Cross, Winchester, and God's House at Portsmouth. He could not be resident in both places at the same time, and in other cases absentee masters lived at the expense of hospital funds for long periods, in some instances hardly ever going there, as happened at Pontefract.

The disillusionment of the common man was paradoxically accompanied by a greater urge towards charitable works by the wealthy, perhaps not so much in order to preserve their own places in heaven, as to guard against civil discontent and upheaval if steps were not taken to restore some social order and balance. The Peasants' Revolt of 1381 might have been abortive in the short term, but it was a sign of things to come.

Whatever the reasons, the late fourteenth and the fifteenth century saw the foundation of some exceptionally well-endowed hospitals and bede-houses in England, as well as an increase in almshouses of secular origin, as men began to look to their own needs more, without depending on the Church.

Some of the earliest hospitals built after the first wave of the dreadful epidemic had passed were in those parts of eastern England which are thought to have been the worst victims. Great Yarmouth acquired two lazar houses in 1349 whilst the Black Death was still wreaking its merciless havoc in East Anglia's chief seaport, and in the following year Ripon and York got new hospitals, both towns having suffered very severely, York perhaps more so as a result of rats overrunning the city after flooding by the Ouse, and spreading the infection more rapidly. Everywhere people were still dying of the pestilence two years after its worst months in 1348.

There was great religious fervour in the immediate wake of the Black Death, since it was generally believed that the disease was visited upon mankind by an angry god. Perhaps those foundations contemporary with the plague were appeasements by men frightened for the safety of their own souls – the pious rich becoming engaged in a sort of medieval alms race – or perhaps they were simply planned before the disaster struck and somehow got built in spite of the social chaos and the sudden labour shortage. Certainly the dearth of new charities for thirty years after the Black Death was broken chiefly in the east, where the plague had first hit Britain with its terror. In 1351 Holbeach got a new hospital, and in the following year, Colchester.

York added to the several charities it already had in 1372 when a clerk, John de Ronclif, started a hospital for thirteen

Sir Richard Whittington – legendary and public-spirited merchant and Lord Mayor of London

poor folk, but his funds were more modest than his ambition, and the foundation had to be rescued in the following century by new endowments by local merchants, eventually becoming a home for ten poor widows maintained by the Merchant Adventurers.

Thirteen poor men and women at Pontefract were given a roof

Whittington's Almshouses, College Hill

over their heads by the foundation of a hospital in 1385 by Sir Robert Knolles, which survived the Dissolution and was granted to the corporation by Elizabeth I.

Arundel, in Sussex, acquired a hospital in about 1380 by the gift of Richard Fitzalan, Earl of Arundel, and it was called by one writer *Domus eleemosynaria*, but was more commonly known as a Maison Dieu. It was to house twenty-four poor old men, and it was a condition of their continued stay that they should not re-marry. The founder was executed in 1395, the foundation dissolved in 1546, and the buildings reduced to ruins by Cromwell's troops in the Civil War.

The Pole family, mentioned in chapter one, was connected with the hospital at Donnington in Berkshire, being credited by some with its foundation. But this establishment can actually be traced back to the reign of Edward II. It was refounded in 1393 by Sir Richard Abberbury, when he also received licence to crenellate Donnington Castle. The link with the Poles is due to Abberbury having sold the estate to Thomas Chaucer, son of the poet, whose daughter Alice was married to William de la Pole, Duke of Suffolk. Both Chaucer and the duke have been credited by different writers with this hospital for thirteen poor men. It was dissolved in 1545, but restored later by Charles Howard, Earl of Nottingham, and the foundation still exists, though now in seventeenth-century brick buildings ranged round a court-yard.

Trinity Hospital at Salisbury is likewise an eighteenth-century brick replacement of medieval buildings erected late in the fourteenth century, the foundation being for twelve poor men. Twelve was the number at Oakham in Rutland, too, where the hospital dedicated to St John and St Anne was founded in 1398 by a merchant, William Dalby, and still exists in the street named after him, and with its original chapel more or less intact. One of the new social developments around this time was a provision for women in childbirth who had nowhere else to go, and Salisbury's Trinity Hospital, among others, specifically catered for 'lying-in women . . . until they are delivered, recovered and churched'. At London's St Bartholomew's and elsewhere it was a rule that, if a woman died in childbirth, her offspring should be brought up in the hospital until it was seven years old.

Coastal towns, meanwhile, were providing for distressed or aged sailors. Hull had its house of alms for poor mariners by 1349, dedicated to the Blessed Trinity, and any Trinity hospital in a port was as probably intended for sailors as an inland one dedicated to St Leonard or St Lazarus was intended wholly or partly for lepers. Of Hull's Trinity Hospital, Defoe wrote in the eighteenth century that it was 'the glory of the town', its revenue increasing 'every day by charities, and bounties of pious minded people', and that it then housed thirty widows of seamen, as well as twelve brethren and six assistants.

How were all these institutions being financed in the medieval period? Some of the larger ones, especially those founded by monarchs, noblemen and bishops, were richly endowed with property from which they made profits in rents or from produce, and the royal foundations, in particular, were likely to receive endowments of money from succeeding monarchs. Allowances of fuel were made from royal forests, too. Henry III granted one oak from Windsor to St Bartholomew's in 1224, and allowed St Leonard's at York to take what it needed for both fuel and building material from the royal forest.

The ruins of St Catherine's Almshouses, Exeter

Charitable institutions were assisted by the holding of fairs, and many individuals left gifts of money to hospitals when they died, usually as insurance against rejection at the golden gates. Tolls called 'thraves' were exacted in the north from landowners, and indulgences were sold by pardoners for the benefit of the poor. Pilgrims moved by superstitious reverence gave money to hospitals such as St Bartholomew's at Oxford, which claimed to possess St Bartholomew's skin, St Stephen's bones, one of St Andrew's ribs, and the comb of Edward the Confessor. The relic which Colet refused to kiss at Canterbury was supposedly a bit of Thomas à Becket's shoe. The giving of alms was strongly encouraged by the Church, and casual donations helped the poorer hospitals to continue.

Sometimes hospitals expected those whom they accepted as inmates to make voluntary contributions on admission, and there were frequent abuses of the system, preference occasionally being given to applicants who could afford to pay. Any property an inmate had was often deemed at his death to be the common property of the hospital.

Not all the hospitals were founded by the rich and mighty, and some of them must have had a hard time making ends meet. At Sandwich, for instance, the hospital of St Thomas was founded in 1392 by a draper, Thomas Ellis, who had twenty-three children to support. As a secular foundation, it survived dissolution, and indeed still exists, though all that is left of the medieval buildings is a stone entrance arch and a traceried window in St Peter's churchyard.

By the end of the fourteenth century, there were no less than 700 charitable foundations throughout England, mostly called 'hospitals', but consisting of lazar houses, infirmaries, asylums, Maisons Dieu, wayfarers' refuges and almshouses in the more modern sense, and all doing their good works without state aid, although sometimes benefiting from royal patronage. The picture Shakespeare gives us of the pathetic Richard II abjectly submitting to Bolingbroke's demands by offering to exchange

> My gorgeous palace for a hermitage,
> My gay apparel for an almsman's gown

Bubwith's rebuilt almshouses at Wells

hardly accords with some of the boy king's actions, but he did leave in his will 6,000 marks* for the maintenance of lepers in London hospitals.

We can open our account of the fifteenth century with the refoundation of St John's at Sevenoaks, Kent, by William Sennocke in 1418. He was a foundling, but became Sir William Sennocke and Lord Mayor of London, and was clearly motivated by altruism rather than by self-interest, for he also founded later a school for the free education of poor children, and provided for twenty poor men and women in the hospital, which was further endowed by Sir John Potkin.

Barnstaple acquired its Holy Trinity Hospital in 1410 when it was a prosperous commercial centre. A few years later came the foundation at Bristol by a merchant of the town, John Barstaple (*sic*) who provided for six poor men and six poor women. This

---

* A mark was a unit of currency which originated in Germany but was common in Western Europe. It represented about thirteen shillings and four pence, or two thirds of a pound.

establishment was also called Trinity Hospital, and survived the Dissolution, Elizabeth I granting it to the corporation.

Around 1417 came what was originally called St Helen's Hospital at Abingdon. It was evidently founded by Geoffrey Barbour and subsequently administered by the Guild of the Holy Cross, which was also responsible for maintaining Abingdon's bridges over the Thames. Six men and six women were housed there before the Dissolution, when the foundation was suppressed, but it was refounded by Sir John Mason in 1553 and named Christ's Hospital, the number of inmates being increased to thirteen. Locally nicknamed Long Alley Almshouses, the sixteenth-century buildings have a long open wooden gallery facing the church, with two porches projecting from it, while the back is of stone and looks on to attractive gardens with clipped yews. Close by are two later groups of almshouses which we shall come to in due course, and which together form a group unique in England.

The ancient muniment chest at Wells

John Streche founded a hospital at Wareham in Dorset in 1418 for 'six antient men and five women' as a surviving inscription records. How did he arrive at these numbers, one wonders? It seems hard luck on one of the men. The foundation survives with a different balance now. The present buildings on the old site date only from 1741, when the almshouses were redesigned in the form of a Georgian house of brick with a belfry, but Streche's beneficiaries no longer live there, having been moved to new modern premises.

Soon after these secular foundations came the Bede House at Higham Ferrers, Northamptonshire. This was founded in traditional enough manner by Henry Chichele, Archbishop of Canterbury, in 1423. Higham Ferrers was his native town, and he provided for twelve bedesmen, none of whom was to be under fifty years old, and the oldest was to be the Prior, responsible for seeing that all the inmates joined in daily evensong, standing at the doors of their cubicles, and obeyed various rules of the house as to their meals, toilet and laundry, among other things. One woman also lived on the premises, as matron, and that perhaps accounts for the minimum age of the men. She should be, the statutes said, 'glad to please every poor man to her power'.

The building was of the usual infirmary hall type, with the chapel at the east end, and was built on the site of an earlier foundation, in alternate courses of brown and white stone, in the parish churchyard, along with the chantry that Archbishop Chichele also built. These buildings remain *in situ*, the bedehouse having served as a Sunday school in recent years, after restoration and the addition of a bellcote to the roof.

In London, that legendary and public-spirited merchant and Lord Mayor, Sir Richard Whittington, among his other charitable works, left money for the building of an almshouse for thirteen poor people, and endowed a refuge at St Thomas's Hospital for young women 'that hadde done a-mysse', instructing that their sins should be kept secret, 'for he wolde not shame no yonge women in no wyse'.

The original almshouse, built in 1424, was in the City, and the Mercers' Hall possesses a contemporary drawing of Whittington on his death-bed, with friends in attendance, and at the foot of the bed, thirteen men representing those for whom he charged his executors 'to ordeyne a house of almes, after his death'.

Preference was to be given to freemen of the Mercers' Company, and they were to pray for the souls of Sir Richard and his wife Alice. The almshouses survived the Dissolution and, unusually, soon afterwards, the Mercers' Company freed the old folk from any obligation to pray for the founder. The foundation survives in Islington, Whittington College having been built there in 1825 in Tudor style round three sides of a courtyard.

Hospital of SS John the Baptist and John the Evangelist at Sherborne, Dorset

Another London hospital was founded on the site of a former synagogue, and dedicated to St Anthony. But it was associated with a school, and a schoolmaster named Johnson, who also became master of the hospital, is said to have 'put out the Almsmen from their houses' and let out the houses for rent, fobbing off the former inmates with twelve pence a week.

At Cirencester, St Thomas's Hospital was founded in 1427 by Sir William Nottingham and was under the patronage of the town's weavers, for it was them the establishment was meant to benefit. It is still in existence, sometimes known as the Weavers' Hall, and it is the oldest secular building in the 'capital of the Cotswolds', built in local stone, naturally.

In Berkshire, the old market town of Thatcham, near

Newbury, was provided with an almshouse in 1433 by Thomas Lowndys, and placed under the management of the parish, in whose care it remains to this day. There is an interesting brass to the founder in the parish church. Barton's Hospital in Buckingham is another foundation of this period, secular in origin, and still in existence after five-and-a-half centuries.

A Recorder of Exeter, William Wynard, founded a 'God's House' in 1436 (the English language having ousted the French in all sections of society by this time). This also had a school attached. The hospital, with its chapel, was known later as Wynard's Hospital, and was for twelve poor men and a chaplain, and still stands, an attractive group of restored red sandstone buildings round a cobbled courtyard, though now used partly as offices. A similar range of buildings known as St Catherine's Almshouses was founded in the same city about 1450, by Canon John Stevens, for thirteen poor men. This ecclesiastical foundation survived the Dissolution, but not the Luftwaffe, German bombing having reduced it to ruin in May 1942. The establishment consisted of chapel, inmates' rooms and refectory round a small courtyard, and the red sandstone ruins have been kept, close to the city centre – a reminder of the

The almshouses at Sherborne in the nineteenth century

medieval look of much of Exeter before the Second World War.
At Wells in Somerset, Nicholas Bubwith, Henry IV's former
Treasurer of England and later Bishop of Bath and Wells, died in
1424 leaving a bequest for the foundation of a hospital for
twenty-four persons, twelve of whom were to be former burgesses of the city and other men and women who were in such
reduced circumstances that they could not pay rent for habi-
tations; and the other twelve so poor that they could not subsist
without alms. The bishop's executors carried out his intentions
in 1436, on a plot of land between what was then Beggar Street
and St Cuthbert's parish churchyard, erecting a hospital in
traditional medieval form, with the chapel and infirmary hall 'al
in length under one Roofe', as Leland described it later.

Much alteration and addition has been made to the medieval
buildings, which probably escaped the general upheaval of the
Reformation in the leniency shown towards Wells on account of
the secular rather than monastic nature of its church. Bishop
Bubwith had given the city a guildhall, which was attached to the
hospital at the opposite end from the chapel, and this was also
converted to almshouse use later, while in the seventeenth
century Bishop Still added further buildings (also posthumously)
along with the striking architectural adornment of the outside
sedilia facing the churchyard – four seats flanked with colon-
nettes and with gabled niches above.

An ancient alms-chest is kept here, standing on an
ornamented pedestal of 1615 bearing the inscription

> In yearle accountes my founder doth will,
> To resite y givft of ye Lord Bushopp Still
> Leaste by neglecte poores payments, in neede
> Be all but in worde and nothing in deede.

One of the residents here told me, lowering his voice and
apologizing to my wife for his language, that four of these
almshouses were intended specifically for homosexuals. If so, it
was a remarkable gesture, for the Church has always unequivo-
cally condemned homosexual practices as sinful, and homosexuals were liable to be put in the pillory and stoned to death by
the mob or, as in the 'tolerant' Netherlands, tied up in a sack and
thrown into the sea.

The year after Bubwith's Almshouses were built at Wells, the Hospital of St John the Baptist and St John the Evangelist was founded at Sherborne in Dorset. This is one of the most remarkable almshouses of the time, in more than one respect, and deserves close attention. Although the Bishop of Salisbury, Robert Neville, interceded with Henry VI for a licence for a board of governors to hold property for the benefit of the poor, the foundation was entirely secular, its building being paid for by the townspeople after a quarrel between the abbey and the town had disrupted Sherborne and led to the townsfolk boycotting the monastic infirmary. The trouble was caused by the monks infringing the townspeople's ancient rights of baptism in the abbey, and the townsmen, as Leland relates, 'rose in playne sedition' and set fire to part of the abbey church. As the bishop had largely supported the monks in this difference, his intercession with the king was no doubt a piece of ecclesiastical diplomacy intended to go some way to restoring the status quo.

The hospital was built close to the abbey in 1437 with money raised among local subscribers, to accommodate 'twelve pore feeble and ympotent old men and four old women'. Although the building followed the usual medieval plan of long infirmary hall with chapel at one end, it was immediately unusual in having two storeys, men being on the ground floor and the women above. The chapel rose through both floors and was consecrated by the new bishop, Ayscough, in 1442.

The hospital then carried on its good work for 400 years with little change, though some of its property was filched at the Dissolution, and in 1593, Sir Walter Raleigh, who then leased Sherborne Castle from the queen, had cause to write to the then master of the hospital, Edward Knoyll, about complaints made to Sir Walter and to Sir Ralph Horsey, whose father had bought the abbey church for the town after the Dissolution, that a poor woman, Eleanor Dyer, had been refused entrance to the hospital. Sir Walter appealed to the master and brethren to restore the woman to her right, so that she should not be 'Dryven further to complain againste them in a mater so unjustly begon and prosecuted by them that are or sholld be protectors and not opresors off poor pepill'.

The residents wore distinctive uniforms – red cloaks and poke bonnets for the women, and blue hats and coats with mitred buttons for the men. They had to take an oath on entry to obey the house rules, and were expected to hear Mass every day. The 'housewife' prepared meals of herrings, apples and figs, did the laundry and made the 'lyttle fether beds'.

Uniform of the women residents at Sherborne – the cloak and bonnet were red

In the 1860s, some expansion took place as a result of a generous benefaction. A new wing was added to the east side, enabling the number of residents to be almost doubled. The architect for this work, William Slater, designed his buildings in Victorian Gothic so well in keeping with the fifteenth-century work, using the same local limestone, that the group now appears as one of the most irresistibly picturesque medieval secular buildings in England. Slater gave the almshouse a new board room above the new living quarters, restored the chapel, and added a new entrance from the east with a delightfully attractive forecourt and cloister with seats where residents can sit in the morning sun. From Half Moon Street and the Abbey Close, one sees Slater's elegant oriel window in the board room flanking the entrance on one side, and on the other, the three-light east window of the chapel with its Perpendicular tracery.

The chapel retains some medieval stained glass in its windows, with the Virgin and the hospital's patron saints, as well as an oak screen and a fifteenth-century Flemish triptych which has the raising of Lazarus as its centrepiece. Also preserved here are the original royal licence and an alms-chest which was ordered to be 'bounden with yren' and to have 'dyvers lokkes and keyes'.

The present population of this almshouse is twenty-one residents and the matron and her assistant, the government being in the hands of a master and twenty brethren, as it has been from medieval times. The residents no longer wear uniforms, but they still take the oath on admittance, and are expected to attend short services in the chapel every Thursday and Friday. Each has his or her own room, there are a few for married couples, and the modern facilities include central heating and a TV room.

A high point in the story of English almshouses was the year 1437. If Sherborne Abbey, with the new hospital and the ancient school where Alfred the Great is thought to have been a pupil, formed a splendid medieval grouping in this old market town, the village of Ewelme in Oxfordshire witnessed the raising of a similar ensemble which, if a little more modest in scale, was quite as extraordinary. It brings us into contact, once again, with the Pole family.

Alice Chaucer, grand-daughter of the poet, inherited the manor of Ewelme in Oxfordshire from her father, Sir Thomas Chaucer, and she and her second husband, William de la Pole, Earl of Suffolk, became powerful favourites of Henry VI and Margaret of Anjou. They feathered their nests in Suffolk and Oxfordshire at the nation's expense, and built a model village at Ewelme around their lavish new palace. They rebuilt the church, and in 1437 founded a school for the education of the village children 'freely, without exaction of any schole hire', and a hospital for thirteen poor men, which was known as God's House. Two chaplains were appointed as masters of the school and the almshouse, and the Chancellor of England was made protector of the revenues, to prevent them from being misappropriated by any future lord of the manor. The school is the oldest free Church school in the country.

The school and the hospital were built of stone, brick and timber, the use of brick being among the earliest in Oxfordshire. The hospital was also one of the earliest quadrangular alms-houses, departing totally from the medieval infirmary hall in having the inmates' two-room lodgings, one room above the other, ranged round a quadrangle with a timber cloister. A gabled timber porch in each side of the cloister gave access from the dwellings to the courtyard, and over one of the doorways is a trefoil design in brick, suggesting that a Flemish craftsman worked here. The roofs were originally thatched, and a covered passage led directly into the adjacent parish church, where the south aisle served as the hospital chapel.

In 1448 the earl became a duke, but two years later he was made the scapegoat for the loss of France, and the king sent him abroad for safety, but hardly had he set sail from Dover when he was seized and thrown into a small boat, where his head was unceremoniously hacked off with a rusty sword and chucked over the side. In the same year, William Ayscough, the Bishop of Salisbury, who had been concerned with the hospital at

Quadrangle of the almshouses at Ewelme, Oxfordshire

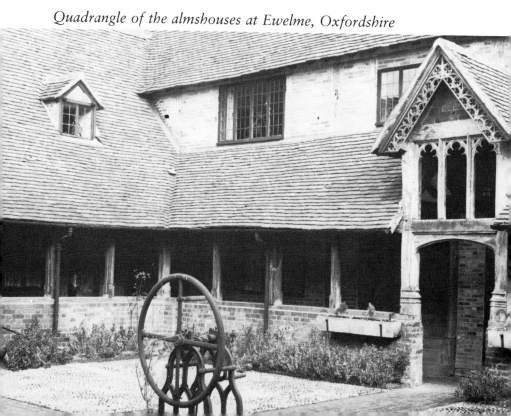

Sherborne, and who, as King Henry's confessor, was held largely responsible for the evils of the royal court, was beaten to death on a hilltop by his congregation at Edington, Wiltshire, after celebrating Mass.

The wealthy and twice-widowed Duchess of Suffolk survived her husband by a quarter of a century, and completed their building projects at Ewelme, richly endowing the hospital, and receiving another rich widow, Margaret of Anjou, into the palace to live with her in lenient confinement. After the death of the duchess, her son John erected the magnificent alabaster monument to her in Ewelme's church, an effigy above showing her in all her finery, wearing her coronet and with the ribbon of the Order of the Garter on her arm; but in the shadows below is an effigy of the half naked and emaciated corpse of the seventy-one-year-old duchess, to remind us that, for all her rapacious accumulation of wealth and power, she is but a dead old woman like the poorest parishioner in the churchyard outside. The almshouse attests to that need to do good works born of the medieval terror of retribution after death, and the founders' statutes made some pious observations and required the inmates to pray regularly for their benefactors' souls, invoking the Lord to have mercy on the souls of 'my lord William sum tyme Duke of Suffolke, and my lady Alice Duchesse of Suffolke his wyfe, oure fyrst fownders', as well as on the souls of the king, the founders' parents, and 'all cristen sowles'. Services began with matins at 6 a.m., and 'if it be so that any of them be so slowthful that the first psalm of matins be begun ere he comes into his stall he shall lose one penny'. The inmates were also expected to 'kepe clene the closter and the quadrate abowte the welle fro wedis and all odyr unclennesse'. Their uniform was a tabard and a hood, with a red cross on the chest.

Henry VIII's commissioners found nothing to criticize in this establishment, and though all the Suffolk estates became Crown property, the almshouse has survived, little changed externally, to the present day, James I having annexed the mastership to the Regius Professor of Medicine at Oxford, with whom it still remains. The cobbled courtyard still has a wellhead at its centre, and the roofs are now tiled, with dormer windows, and tall brick chimney stacks are on the outside of the square. The foundation's revenues provided sufficient funds for a recent interior

The tomb of Alice Chaucer, Duchess of Suffolk, in Ewelme church

modernization which now provides self-contained maisonettes.

Eton College was founded by the pious Henry VI partly as a hospital in 1440, twenty-four poor infirm men to be accommodated as well as the poor scholars and the schoolmaster, clerks and choristers. But it was hardly thirty years old before the almshouses were swamped out of existence by the growing school. Shrewsbury's prosperous wool drapers built St Mary's around 1444 with money provided by Degory (?Gregory) Watur, and the foundation still exists as Drapers' Almshouses, though the present buildings are of nineteenth-century brick, and mock-Tudor in style. The townsmen of Northampton, too, founded a hospital around 1450, dedicated to St Thomas-a-Becket, whose trial took place at Northampton Castle. The foundation still exists.

At Dartford in 1453 we come across one of the first foundations which had 'alms house' as its actual title as opposed to 'hospital'. The king granted a licence to four men, John Bamburgh, William Rothele, Roger Jones and Thomas Boost, to erect a hospital for five poor people which was to be named Trinity Alms House. The vicar and churchwardens of the town were to be its governors, but it seems that the establishment did not survive the Dissolution, for we have no trace of it after the middle of the sixteenth century. It is worth noting that the dedication of the parish church is to the Holy Trinity, and that it contains a brass to Joan, wife of William Rothele, she having died in 1464. No doubt the church also served as the chapel for the modest gathering of almsmen.

At Burford in Oxfordshire, the so-called 'Great Almshouses' claim to have been founded by Richard, Earl of Warwick, in 1457, but the Bishop of Burford is entitled to the chief credit, the earl only having granted the land as lord of the manor. Although much altered in the nineteenth century, the building remains externally medieval, built of stone close to the parish church with roofs of graded stone tiles.

Thomas Jackenett founded an almshouse at Cambridge in 1469 which remains, now combined with the later Wray charity, and Heytesbury in Wiltshire acquired its St John's Hospital in 1472 by virtue of the gift of Lord Hungerford, Edward IV's Lord High Treasurer, and it was further endowed by his descendants, but the buildings were burnt down in Heytesbury's disastrous fire of 1769. The charity provided for twelve poor men and one woman, with a custodian who had to be a clerk in holy orders, acting as chaplain also. The rebuilt hospital is of brick round three sides of a turfed square, with the Hungerford family arms over the gabled entrance and a clock and bell turret above.

In London, evidence that leprosy had not yet completely disappeared by the late Plantagenet period comes from Holloway, where a hospital wholly for lepers was founded in 1473 by one William Pole, a yeoman who was himself a victim of leprosy, on land granted by Edward IV for the purpose. And at Knightsbridge, yet another lazar house was erected, probably about the same time and at the instigation of the king, for reference is made in a record of 1475 to a vicar from a royal manor in Norfolk having fallen victim to leprosy and being an inmate 'in the Spitell house of knygtyes brygge beside Westminster'. This place was dedicated to St Leonard.

We have not had occasion to consider Derbyshire so far in this survey, but the county comes to our notice in a curious way, for

A corner of the inner courtyard at Browne's Hospital

there is a record of Walter Blount, Lord Mountjoy, having founded in 1474 a hospital for seventeen poor men at Bentley, between the village and Alkmonton. The men were to be over fifty-five years of age, with gowns and hoods provided, and were to pray for the souls of their benefactor and his family and several prominent lords of the realm. But where *was* this hospital? Was it at Hungry Bentley, a village now totally lost, and the nearest Bentley to Alkmonton? Who knows? Wherever this hospital was, it is not there now.

Nor is the Maison Dieu founded at Northallerton in North Yorkshire in 1476 for thirteen poor men and women. This was the creation of a local draper, Richard de Moore, and its secular origin made it safe from suppression. Indeed, it seems to have survived until the nineteenth century, when it was under the patronage of the Earl of Carlisle.

Yeovil's hospital of St George and St Christopher the Martyrs was founded in 1477 by J. Wobourne, who laid down that the pensioners were to wear red crosses on their breasts in honour of St George, 'patron of the house of alms'. The foundation still exists, its buildings in Bond Street now known as Woborn's Almshouses.

The stone-built Gardiner's Almshouses in Lancaster, though largely rebuilt in the eighteenth century, were originally founded in 1485, and were possibly the last of strictly medieval origin, for that was the year of Bosworth, but political events did not have any immediate effects on local charities, which were still born of medieval habits of mind, and I will continue this chapter with the charitable foundations of Henry VII's reign.

Browne's Hospital at Stamford in Lincolnshire, for instance, the chapel of which was consecrated in 1494, was no revolutionary establishment of the Tudor age, but a thoroughly medieval concept in both its purpose and its architecture. It was founded some time in the 1480s by William Browne, a local merchant of the Staple of Calais, and of 'a very wonderful Richenesse', as John Leland tells us, Browne being an alderman and thrice Sheriff of Rutland. A large brass to Browne and his wife in Stamford's parish church shows him standing on two woolpacks. He was also anxious to perpetuate his own name, leaving directions in his will that the bede-house he founded should remain for ever 'for the invocation of the most glorious Virgin

The nineteenth-century gatehouse of the medieval foundation at Lambourn, Berkshire

Mary and All Saints'. William Browne died in 1489, the buildings still unfinished, but the work was carried on and further endowed by his brother-in-law, Thomas Stoke, who was a chaplain to the Lord Chancellor. They followed the medieval arrangement of dormitory hall with apartments for twelve poor men, and chapel in one long range, built in keeping with the rest of this stylish town of limestone. As at Sherborne in Dorset, however, there were two storeys, the chapel rising through both. The upper floor was an audit room, where the hospital's accounts were kept and inspected annually.

This hospital has undergone much alteration over the centuries, including its enlargement into a range of rooms and offices round an open courtyard with a cloister on one side, and the addition of a clock tower to the main building. The original cubicles of the bedesmen were removed in the modernization programme, when two women 'advanced in age' were admitted in addition to the ten men.

Ludlow's Hosyer's Almshouses were founded in 1486 and were under the patronage of the religious guild of the Palmers, of which John Hosyer was a member. There were thirty-three rooms each with its own wall fireplace – still generally a luxury, central floor hearths being the custom for the poor for some time yet. At the Dissolution, the borough corporation took over the suppressed guild's properties, including the grammar school it had founded, as well as the almshouses, but both were subsequently rebuilt, the latter in brick in 1758.

In 1492, the Seamen's Guild at Newcastle-on-Tyne built its Trinity Almshouses, the foundation surviving but the present buildings dating only from the eighteenth century. What a contrast these relatively grand buildings were to the tiny and curious half-timbered house in the churchyard at Itchingfield in Sussex. It was built originally in the fifteenth century as a house for a travelling priest to stay in, but became an almshouse at the end of the century; a very quiet home for some old person of the village, shaded by the churchyard yews. Alas, it is now boarded up and derelict.

Lambourn in Berkshire acquired an almshouse for ten poor men around 1500, by the gift of John Estbury, whose tomb with a brass is in the church, where the almsmen gathered to say a prayer for his soul every day. In the early nineteenth century, the funds allowed a pension to each inmate of twenty-two shillings a week, plus an annual allowance of free wood, wheat and malt, but the old almshouses were completely rebuilt in the second half of the century.

The Hospital of St John the Baptist still exists at Lichfield, and though largely rebuilt, some parts of the medieval buildings remain, in particular the almost factory-like row of eight huge chimney breasts of the east range, facing St John Street. This hospital was refounded in 1495 by Bishop William Smyth on the site of an earlier (probably twelfth century) bishop's foundation. Bishop Smyth was also the founder of Brasenose College at Oxford, and his good works led Thomas Fuller to aver that 'this man wheresoever he went may be followed by the perfume of charity he left behind him'.

A rector of Stevenage, Stephen Hellard, founded the All Christian Soul House there in 1501, and it remains in the care of the town, now re-named after its founder, whose memorial brass is in the parish church, showing him in his vestments.

Another guild hospital was founded at Coventry in 1507 by Thomas Bond, a draper and mayor of the town, and dedicated to the Holy Trinity, the eleven poor inmates (ten men, one woman) bearing an identifying badge on their gowns. It was built on two floors, with the dormitories above the hall and kitchen, and the upper half-timbered structure overhanging the lower, built of stone. It still exists, and even some of the original buildings remain, though much restored in the nineteenth century, and sometimes called Bablake Hospital on account of its close later association with a boys' school of that name. They form a little corner of medieval Coventry that survived the 1940 blitz. In 1619, one of the inmates here, named Johnson, was accused of murdering eight of his fellow inmates by giving them rat poison, in order to gain the extra privileges of being the senior brother. He then poisoned himself, and was buried in the customary manner for suicides – at a crossroads with a stake through his heart.

The foundation in 1506 of a hospital at Brough, in what was then Westmorland, deserves notice, for that was a region apparently so remote as to be beyond the pale as far as Christian charity was concerned. It was a sparsely populated area, however, and this tiny establishment, having only two beds, was

The Victorian courtyard of the rebuilt Lambourn almshouses

intended by its founder, John Brunskill (who also gave the parish church its bells), mainly for travellers across the inhospitable Pennines near the Yorkshire border – perhaps used most by pilgrims on the way to York. Hospital chapels were built only with the permission of the bishops, and on condition that they did not interfere with the parochial system. They were often not allowed to have a bell, in case its tolling drew outsiders to worship there instead of in the parish church; and at Brough a dispute blew up with the local vicar when the chantry with which the diminutive hospital was associated begot rumours of miracles and itself became a place of pilgrimage, though not for long. Superstition, and with it good charitable work, was about to be stamped *on*, if not *out*.

For the time being, however, as medieval England gradually gave way to the Tudor view of society, pious philanthropists continued to derive comfort, as they gave their money away, from the oft-quoted verses of *Matthew* 25: 'For I was an hungred, and ye gave me meat: I was thirsty, and ye gave me drink: I was a stranger, and ye took me in: Naked, and ye clothed me: I was sick, and ye visited me: I was in prison, and ye came unto me'. These wealthy founders did not, on the other hand, take to heart the advice of Christ in the Sermon on the Mount. Alert as they apparently were to *Matthew* 25, they seem to have been either ignorant or dismissive of *Matthew* 6: 'Take heed that ye do not your alms before men, to be seen of them: otherwise ye have no reward of your Father which is in heaven. Therefore when thou doest thine alms, do not sound a trumpet before thee, as the hypocrites do in the synagogues and in the streets, that they may have glory of men'. . . .

Even those who were inclined to heed this advice had more than pure compassion to motivate them in their charitable works. It was universally believed throughout Christendom before the Reformation that failure to be charitable to the needy would result in vicious torments in purgatory, and those rich men who did not found almshouses were inclined to leave money for doles to be handed out to the poor, often at their funerals, when the recipients could thank them with their prayers, for the prayers of the poor were considered effective in relieving the pains of purgatory.

It is, of course, all too easy to be cynical about the motives of

A former almshouse in the churchyard at Itchingfield, West Sussex

philanthropists, and whilst there is no reason to blind ourselves to these motives (especially as the philanthropists did not often do so themselves), we must recognize at the same time that the money and property these benefactors gave to the poor did an immeasurable amount of good, and continues to do so in an amazing number of cases, centuries after the givers have all but faded into oblivion.

3 The Tudor Call to Alms

In 1509, the last year of Henry VII, the king resolved to restore the great but decayed Savoy Palace in London as a hospital for a hundred poor people. Built by Simon de Montfort in 1245 beside the Thames, it was named after Peter, Count of Savoy, to whom it had been granted by Henry III. King John of France had died in this palace, Chaucer was probably married there, and Wycliff had preached in it. It was said to be the finest palace in the kingdom, and full of more riches than any other in Christendom, but during the Peasants' Revolt of 1381 it was burned down by the mob. It had lain in ruins for more than 120 years when Henry Tudor conceived his plan to turn it into a monument to his generosity and the kindness of his heart, for, as he said, 'there be fewe or noon such commune Hospitalls within this our Realme, and that for lack of them, infinite nombre of pouer nedie people miserably dailly die, no man putting hande of helpe or remedie'. Actually, this was hardly true, but it was good propaganda for the king's saintliness when, as he was shortly to do, he met his maker. As he said in his will, the works of 'Charite and Mercy bee moost profitable, due and necessarie for the salvation of man's soule. . . . We therefor of our great pitie and compassion . . .' etc. He *said* he intended to build similar hospitals in York and Coventry, but they never materialized.

The Savoy Hospital was built, however, at a cost of 10,000 marks, on a cruciform plan, and dedicated to St John the Baptist. The building took eight years, being opened in 1517, and although it did not escape close enquiry from Henry VIII's commissioners, it survived until 1553 when it was suppressed by the founder's sickly grandson, Edward VI, shortly before his death, for by then it had become little more than a dosshouse for vagabonds and disreputable women, and although it was re-endowed by Mary Tudor, it never again fulfilled its royal

Porch of Greenway's Almshouses, Tiverton

founder's charitable purposes. It was an ominous beginning for the House of Tudor's concern for the nation's poor and needy.

Elsewhere in the kingdom, though, things went on much as before, well into the reign of Henry VIII. While the new king was settling himself into the vacant throne, the Abbot of Glastonbury, Richard Beere's refounded almshouse at Taunton, originally a twelfth-century lazar house, was being done up, with his arms on the front, bearing his initials beneath his abbot's mitre. The old building remains, thatched among a congregation of council houses, but is no longer an almshouse. The same abbot – a prolific builder – founded an almshouse at Glastonbury itself in 1512, close to the abbey. It was for women only, and has long gone, but the old gateway with the arms of Henry VIII remains on the redeveloped site.

Hull added to its already impressive collection of charitable institutions in 1513 with St James's, and Exeter followed with an almshouse founded by one of the prominent local family of Fortescues.

At Leicester, meanwhile, William Wyggeston was building a hospital similar in style to Browne's at Stamford and St John's at Sherborne, with twelve men on one floor and twelve women on the other. It was dedicated to St Ursula and St Catherine. Wyggeston was one of Leicester's greatest benefactors, a rich wool merchant and twice the town's mayor, who founded schools as well as the hospital. He owned nearly a quarter of all the taxable property in Leicester, and endowed the hospital with land that was later part of the Leicestershire coalfield, and thus greatly increased the value of the endowment. His statue in gown and ruff is one of those on the city's Victorian clock tower. His foundation still exists, but the old buildings facing the church which became the city's cathedral were demolished, amid much protest, in 1868, and new ones built further from the centre, another rebuilding taking place as recently as 1968. The master of the almshouse is appointed by the Chancellor of the Duchy of Lancaster, as with the town's Trinity Hospital discussed earlier.

John Taylor, the so-called 'water poet', visiting Leicester about a century after the completion of Wyggeston's original hospital, wrote that the people of Leicester were 'so charitable and careful in providing for the poor and needy that a man must go seek where to bestow his alms, for there is not anyone (that I could see) that begged in the whole town'. Around 1700 Celia Fiennes reported 'two Hospitalls, one for old men ye other women 24 in number; they are allowed 2s. 8d. pr weeke, Candle, fewell, oatmeale, butter and salt'.

Another wealthy wool merchant of the time was John Greenway of Tiverton in Devon, one of the nouveaux riches, who founded the almshouse named after him in about 1517. He also spent lavishly on the town's parish church. The almshouse buildings of red sandstone were, unusually, of three storeys, but with the usual chapel at the end. The latter has a fine porch on to the street with very worn but still visible coats of arms and shields carved on it, and beneath the cornice of the building is carved the inscription: 'Have grace ye men and pray for the sowl of John and Jone Grenway'. John and his wife Joan were much concerned for their own salvation, as is clear from their image in the church, but William Wyggeston at Leicester, too, had founded a chantry before his hospital. The fear that it is 'easier for a camel to go through the eye of a needle, than for a rich man to enter the kingdom of God' continued to weigh heavily on men who were still essentially medieval in spirit and anxious to follow Christ's injunction to 'lay up for yourselves treasures in heaven'. John Greenway's foundation and his original buildings still exist, but the latter are very decayed and his modern beneficiaries are housed in new cottages.

At about the same time, William Ford – yet another rich wool merchant – founded a hospital at Coventry for five poor men and one woman, with five pence a week each provided for their maintenance. The place was called Greyfriars Hospital, and was in reality a bede-house, since the inmates were required to pray for the souls of William Ford, Henry and William Pisford, and their wives, and a priest was provided to say Mass twice a week.

William Pisford was Ford's executor, and he extended the foundation to take in six married couples, increasing their allowance to sevenpence-halfpenny per couple and the same for the resident nurse or matron, who was to be between forty and fifty years old, and whose customary duties were to make sure the inmates and their homes were kept clean, and to see to their food and laundry. If a woman inmate died before her husband,

Courtyard of the restored Ford's Hospital at Coventry

Row of almshouses at Henley-on-Thames built by John Longland, Bishop of Lincoln, in 1547 and rebuilt later

the widower would still receive the full 7½d, but if the man died first, the widow would only receive half that sum!

The buildings were erected round a small narrow and completely enclosed courtyard, and were oak framed like so much of medieval Coventry. The street front had three richly carved gables and oriel windows, with the upper storey sticking out over the pavement at the bottom of Greyfriars Lane. The courtyard was embellished with foliage carving and ornamental bargeboards. The whole was a very fine example of medieval craftsmanship. The inmates lived on either side of the courtyard, with their bedrooms on the upper floors, and there was a common hall at one end and a chapel at the other, over the entrance doorway. The inmates had a little common garden at the back.

There has been much talk of miracles at Coventry in modern times, and for those who believe in them, Ford's Hospital, as it is now called, must be counted among them. It somehow survived Tudor dissolution, in spite of its religious constitution, but then fell foul of James I, who sold the forfeited estates to the city. Subsequently, changes were made to accommodate women only, some secular recompense for medieval discrimination against them in a city which had once been visited, according to legend, by virgins from Cologne bearing gifts of 11,000 virtues for all succeeding generations of Coventry women. But in October 1940 a less welcome tribe came from Germany bearing tons of high explosives, and Ford's Hospital was very badly damaged in the bombing. The matron's room received a direct hit, and she and seven other women were killed. After the war, repairs were put in hand and modern craftsmen painstakingly restored the buildings to their present splendid condition, so that, though mauled, they remain to all of us, and not just to the pensioners, a 'perfect gem of domestic architecture' as Rotha Mary Clay wrote in 1909.

At Cullompton, Devon; Layer Marney, Essex; Childrey, Berkshire (now in Oxfordshire), and in and around London, new almshouses were founded in the 1520s, whilst Luther stirred up dissent abroad and the king began his long quarrel with the Church at home. Sir George Monoux, a member of the Drapers' Company and Lord Mayor of London, built the Monoux Almshouses at Walthamstow in 1527 for thirteen poor people. The foundation remains, but the present red brick buildings date from the eighteenth century.

One or two hospitals were built in the early 1530s and in the 1540s; at Henley-on-Thames, for instance, in 1547, where John Longland, Bishop of Lincoln, built a row along the west side of the churchyard, still in existence though rebuilt; some were built at Chester in 1532, preference there being given to the widows of aldermen. Soon after Henry VIII had suppressed the smaller religious houses in 1536, a mayor of Exeter, John Gilberd, founded at Newton Bushell (now Newton Abbot) a hospital 'for the releff of powre lazar-people, whereof grete nomber with that diseas be now infectid in that partis, to the grete daunger of infection of moche people'. The Southwest seems to have been the last stronghold of leprosy in England, and this was almost certainly the last hospital founded specifically for lepers. The foundation still exists as Gilberd's Almshouses.

The effect of the Dissolution on such charitable foundations was sudden and dramatic. Hardly a single new hospital or almshouse was built in England for more than thirty years. Moreover, a great many poor who already lived in such foundations were thrown out on the streets. This was most likely when the places were attached to chantries or religious guilds, or were ecclesiastical in origin, or bede-houses. Few escaped close scrutiny, and those with the best chances of survival were those secular houses which were too poorly endowed to be worth bothering about. In many cases, as we have seen, hospitals were confiscated from the Church but allowed to remain as useful charitable institutions, often being sold to the towns they stood in. But York lost St Leonard's, London temporarily lost St Bartholomew's and others permanently, including later the Savoy, notwithstanding its royal foundation; and many other towns suddenly found a great increase in the number of beggars in their streets. The charity of the monks was sorely missed, for as one contemporary complained in 1546: 'the pore impotent creatures (had) some relefe of theyr scrappes, where as nowe they have nothyng. Then they had hospitals, and almshouses to be lodged in, but nowe they lye and starve in the stretes'.

Around 1536 Robert Copland wrote *The hye way to the Spyttell hous.* In sheltering from a snow storm in the porch of a hospital, he got into conversation with the porter, and his poem is a picture of the situation at one hospital, generally thought to be St Bartholomew's, at about the time of its dissolution. I have modernized the spelling and punctuation in this instance. After observing that:

> . . . I have seen at sundry hospitals
> That many have lain dead without the walls,
> And for lack of succour have died wretchedly
> Unto your foundation I think contrary . . .

the author asks the porter who is admitted to the hospital and who turned away. The porter answers:

> Forsooth, they that be at such mischief
> That for their living can do no labour,
> And have no friends to do them succour:
> As old people sick and impotent,
> Poor women in childbed have here easement,

Weak men sore wounded by great violence
And sore men eaten with pox and pestilence;
And honest folk fallen in great poverty
By mischance or other infirmity;
Wayfaring men and maimed soldiers
Have they relief in this poor house of ours,
And all other which we deem good and plain
Have here lodging for a night or twain.
Bedrid folk, and such as cannot crave,
In these places most relief they have;
And if they hap within our place to die,
Then they are buried well and honestly.
But not every unsick stubborn knave,
For then we should over many have.

How disastrous the Dissolution was in increasing the burden
of homeless poor can perhaps be inferred from the example of
Bury St Edmunds, which had no less than five medieval hospitals, all of them outside the old town gates. As well as St
Saviour's, already discussed, and situated outside the North
Gate, there was St Petronilla's outside the South Gate, St Peter's,
founded as a lazar house by Abbot Anselm in the twelfth
century, outside the Risby Gate, and the hospitals of St Nicholas
and St John the Evangelist, both thirteenth-century foundations,
outside the East Gate. All these were lost, though the lepers at St
Peter's (if there were any left) seem to have been rehoused,
probably so as to protect the public from them. Although Bury St
Edmunds has made up in more recent times for its losses, few
traces remain of the medieval foundations that distinguished the
old town.

The charges made against the hospitals by Henry's commissioners to justify their suppression were mainly on grounds
of superstition and vagrancy when they were not included in the
general condemnation of the monasteries on grounds of corruption and immorality. The new Protestant doctrine laid down
that good works could not atone for a life of luxury; that the rich
could not bargain with God for a seat in Paradise. And the
Protestant ethic came down heavily on what it saw as malinger-
ing. 'If a man will not work,' St Paul had said, 'neither shall he
eat'. There were, of course, all sorts of dodges whereby those not

Lord Leycester's Hospital, Warwick

entitled to them could get free board and lodging. Men came to the doors of almshouses pretending to be old soldiers or ship-wrecked sailors, or made their mouths foam with soap, or claimed to be lame or otherwise incapacitated.

There was undoubtedly as much corruption among the masters and staff of hospitals as among the abbots and monks of the monasteries. Many cases are recorded of masters misusing funds, and at York one was convicted for taking in more people than were strictly provided for, most of them being admitted for a payment which the master pocketed. At St Thomas's, Canter-bury, a man was convicted for fraudulently receiving money intended for the hospital's use; at Carlisle a master 'dissipated and consumed the goods and alienated the lands to the great decay of the hospital'; at Stamford a master defrauded the poor of their alms; a man who had lost both legs was charged six shillings and eightpence for a bed at Gloucester; and at St Leonard's, York, one master made 500 marks a year from traffic in pensions. Founders frequently took the precaution of laying down strict rules to prevent masters from being absent for long periods or neglecting their duties, or frequenting alehouses or going hunting, not to mention other infamous vices. The Duke and Duchess of Suffolk, in ordering frequent inspection at Ewelme, had observed that 'Diverse places of almesse . . . have bene by Myslyvyng and negligence ybought to grete hevynesse and at the last to grete desolacon'. No wonder the social critic and former friar Henry Brinkelow wrote in 1536: 'I heare that the masters of your hospitals be so fat that the pore be kept leane and bare inough'.

Henry VIII enacted new laws against vagrancy which allowed able-bodied beggars to be whipped and/or put in the stocks, and the ten-year-old Edward VI passed a law in the first year of his reign permitting sturdy beggars to be made slaves for two years and to be branded on their chests with a 'V' (for 'vagrant'). This Act was repealed two years later, but Elizabeth I continued the hard Tudor line against convicted vagabonds, who could be burned through their right ears or otherwise mutilated, or whipped until the blood ran down their backs, then returned to their places of origin, where they were to be lodged in alms-houses if considered incapable of work for any reason.

King Henry's commissioners permitted the continuation of

the custom at St Cross, Winchester, of providing daily meals for a hundred poor, on condition that the food and drink was given only to those who 'study and labour with all their strength at handywork to obtain food; and in no case shall such alms be afforded to strong, robust and indolent mendicants, like so many that wander about such places, who ought rather to be driven away with staves, as drones and useless burdens upon the earth'.

The Reformation bred fear and loathing of the wilfully idle in England hardly exceeded by the horror of Communists in the modern United States. The poor were feared as a source of sedition, crime and disease, to say nothing of witchcraft, and their relief was as much a matter of state security as of pity. In the early years after the Dissolution, the situation was desperate. The old, the sick and the unemployed had lost their only help, which was from the Church, and they 'lie in the streets as is commonly seen and are permitted to die like dogs or beasts without mercy'. In London, innumerable poor people were forced to go, as Brinkelow put it, 'from dore to dore, and to syt openly in the stretes a beggynge'. The Pilgrimage of Grace (1536), that great northern demonstration against the suppression of the monasteries and the termination of their good works, was cruelly crushed.

Those who proposed the redistribution of the Church's wealth to aid the poor were disappointed. Henry Brinkelow, the former friar who wrote ballads under the pseudonym Roderigo Mors, advocated that 'certain houses be maintained, to lodge and kepe pore men in, such as be not able to labour, syck, sore, blind and lame, and every one of them to have wherwith to live, and to have poore whole women to minister unto them', and he suggested further that physicians and surgeons should be appointed in every town to attend to the poor without taking a penny from them, 'uppon payne of lousing both his eares and his stipend also'. This vision of a National Health Service was not heeded. Sir Thomas More had envisaged old-age pensions in his *Utopia*, and the Protestant bishops Latimer and Ridley were advocates of the use of the Church's wealth for the benefit of the poor. But all these seeds of social conscience fell on stony ground.

At the end of his life, however, Henry VIII, 'divine mercy

inspiring us', as he put it, listened to local supplications and granted letters patent in which he styled himself creator and founder of the reopened St Bartholomew's, having evidently read *Matthew* 25, for he intended, he said, that 'henceforth there be comfort to the prisoners, shelter to the poor, visitation to the sick, food to the hungry, drink to the thirsty, clothes to the naked, and sepulture to the dead administered there'. How touching are his tender feelings!

He and Edward VI allowed some other hospitals to be reopened, readily giving their names if not their money to such charities, and in the last year of Edward's reign Christ's Hospital was founded by the king for fatherless children – the famous 'Bluecoat School', built on the site of a suppressed Franciscan priory in the City of London.

In 1551 a merchant of Ipswich, Henry Tooley, left a bequest for almshouses and a hospital for the sick in the town. He was buried in the church of St Mary at the Quay, which was then only a hundred years old, and was subsequently a victim of bombing in the Second World War. Thirty years after his death the almshouses accommodated forty poor folk. They were rebuilt in the nineteenth century in what is now called Foundation Street, and the foundation still exists as Tooley's Court.

At Wimborne Minster in Dorset, Lady Gertrude Courtenay founded a hospital, leaving money for its endowment in her will of 1557, the same year that Sir John Port died, leaving money for the foundation of a hospital at Etwall in Derbyshire, an attractive group round a square courtyard. The inmates here were to be selected from the 'poor, needy and impotent' of Etwall.

Around this time at Thame in Oxfordshire, Lord Williams, the lord of the manor who had been one of the king's agents in dissolving the monasteries, taking for himself all the best Church property in the county, and then served Mary Tudor in the burning of Cranmer, Ridley and Latimer, redeemed himself somewhat by refounding almshouses built at Thame in 1460 as a bede-house by Richard Quatremain. The tombs of both are in the parish church, and Quatremain records his foundation of 'a chantrie, vi pore men and a fraternitye, In the worship of Seynt Cristofore to be relevid in perpetuyte'. Lord Williams built six brick and timber cottages with an overhanging gable end in the

Tudor ornamentation in the courtyard at Warwick

town's high street, and no doubt met his maker soon afterwards with a clearer conscience.

Hardly any other Catholic philanthropist felt Mary Tudor's succession to be secure enough to risk works of charity that might turn out to be money down the drain, and the poor beggars in the streets remained largely uncared for until the Elizabethan Poor Laws set about putting the poor to work and introducing compulsory poor rates in place of voluntary almsgiving. Some of the larger towns had already exacted taxes for poor-relief before it became the law of the land, and town and parish councils, faced with rising populations and increasing poverty, gradually took over the responsibilities for their poor, to compensate for the collapse of religious charity. It has been estimated that, in London, 45% of charity went for religious purposes before the Reformation; only 7% after it.

One of the long-term results of the Dissolution was that almshouses were founded in villages and small towns as well as in the cathedral cities and monastic settlements where they had been chiefly concentrated before. At Drewsteignton, Devon, Peter Edgcumbe, who died in 1546, left to the parish a tiny granite house, against which the churchyard lychgate leans. It dates from earlier in the century, and has been used as an almshouse ever since, though now due to be replaced.

The reign of Elizabeth had run half its course before major private benefactions began to appear again as a result of more settled times and policies. One of the leaders in the field was the queen's favourite, Robert Dudley, Earl of Leicester, who founded in 1571 a hospital at Warwick which he called, reverting perversely to the French of the old aristocracy, a 'Maison Dieu'. But we cannot complain too much about the earl's choice of name, as we equally perversely and unaccountably retain outdated spelling in calling it today Lord Leycester's Hospital.

Some of the buildings date from the fifteenth century, having belonged to the Guilds of Holy Trinity and St George, just inside the town's west gate, over which the guilds' chapel stood. The combined guilds fell foul of the king at the Dissolution, and the property was conveyed to Robert Dudley by the town. The chapel was built of stone, but the rest of the buildings were timber-framed, and the earl's additions turned them into a spectacular black-and-white ensemble with highly picturesque gables and decorative details, overhanging first floors and steeply pitched roofs. The courtyard is particularly attractive, with its lavish woodcarving, coats of arms, a covered exterior staircase, and along one side a cloistered passage with a gallery above it. This hospital for twelve poor men, preferably local old soldiers, was richly endowed, and by virtue of its income from extensive estates, an Act of Parliament of 1813 granted each inmate eighty pounds a year. They formerly wore gowns of blue cloth with silver badges.

Gifts of land to charities that were intended to continue in perpetuity were infinitely more valuable than gifts of money. Cash endowments and legacies were devalued by soaring inflation, and the hospitals with the largest revenues were those which owned land and property.

Winchcombe (Gloucester), Long Melford (Suffolk) and Ross-on-Wye (Hereford) were among towns with new almshouses being built in the early 1570s. Winchcombe's were founded in 1573 by Lady Dorothy Chandos for twelve old folk, and still exist, though much restored, set back from the main street with the arms of the Chandos family of Sudeley Castle carved on them at each end and a gargoyle in the middle of the mossy-roofed row of stone.

Long Melford's Trinity Hospital was built in the same year and had equally aristocratic origins. Sir William Cordell of Melford Hall, Speaker of the House of Commons and Master of the Rolls, founded it for twelve poor men and two poor women, and erected a large and impressive building of red brick which, though much rebuilt in the nineteenth century, remains to us, with a cupola above the centre of a long range flanked by gabled projections. It stands on the green near the parish church, its grounds enclosed by a brick wall.

Ross-on-Wye's Rudhall Almshouses came two years later, a much more modest affair of red sandstone with mullioned windows.

The Drapers' Company's Queen Elizabeth College at Greenwich was founded in 1547 by William Lambarde, and has been claimed as the first such charitable institution to be built after the Reformation. In London it may have been, but the claim was obviously made in ignorance of what was happening in the provinces. Lambarde was a jurist and antiquary, author of

A Perambulation of Kent, and in 1600, the year before his death, he was appointed Keeper of the Records at the Tower of London. His almshouses were rebuilt in 1819, with cottages round three sides of a courtyard and a chapel in the middle of the main range.

In 1579 two new foundations arose at Rochester and Tiverton. Watts's Charity Hospital at Rochester is more commonly known as the 'Poor Travellers' House'. It was founded under the will of Richard Watts, a local merchant, for 'six poor travellers who not being rogues or proctors may receive gratis, for one night, lodging, entertainment, and four pence each', as an inscription on the building states. Charles Dickens reported on this establishment in *Household Words* and said that the property bequeathed for its maintenance had been marshland at the time of the founder's death, but that its value was greatly

The extraordinary circular building at Beamsley in North Yorkshire

increased, having been reclaimed and built upon. The hospital itself still stands, though twice partly rebuilt, on three storeys with a thrice gabled façade of ashlar stonework.

Sixty-two years after Greenway's Almshouses at Tiverton came Waldron's, likewise the foundation of a rich merchant, and if it were not that the passage of time must have put such workmanship beyond the former mason's hand, we should be inclined to say it was built by the same man. John Waldron's chapel porch was clearly modelled very closely on John Greenway's, having a Gothic arch with drip-mould instead of the round arch of the earlier establishment, but otherwise similarly embellished with arms and shields and built of the same red sandstone. The houses themselves were reached from a wooden gallery. The new almshouses were for eight poor old men who were to receive two shillings a week each, milk money of eight shillings a year, and an annual new year gift of twelve and sixpence. The foundation still exists, but modern flats have taken the place of the much-restored old buildings, which were not completed until 1597, after the founder's death, for as an inscription on the stonework recorded in attributing the foundation to 'John Walrond (sic) and Richord his wife': 'At such tyme as the walls were fourtyne foote hye he departed this world even the eyghtynth of July 1597'.

Whilst Waldron's buildings were going up at Tiverton, another almshouse, which seems almost like a space-age vision compared with Tiverton's even then slightly old-fashioned Gothic, was being erected at Beamsley in Yorkshire (then in the West Riding, now in North Yorkshire). Margaret Russell, Countess of Cumberland, founded the Beamsley Hospital in 1593, but its present shape was evidently given it about sixty years later by the redoubtable Anne Clifford, Countess of Pembroke, who finished it 'more profusely'. Behind the two-storey range fronting the road, with a gatehouse flanked by three dwellings on either side, is a circular building with a chapel in the centre and seven rooms round it, with four chimney stacks on the walls between them and the chapel. This extraordinary building has been sold to the Landmark Trust, and the residents are to be rehoused at Skipton.

Another house of pity that looked architecturally rather different from the norm of the time was built at St Germans,

Cornwall, by Sir Walter Moyle. It consisted of six houses with projecting gables supported on rude stone piers, forming a loggia on the ground floor with a balcony above, and providing accommodation for twelve poor people. This interesting range has been restored recently after being empty and neglected for some years.

Robert Johnson, the archdeacon who founded the schools in the Midlands at Oakham and Uppingham in 1584, also founded almshouses in both towns, though at Uppingham the highly successful school eventually took over the original buildings in the course of expansion.

At Rothwell in Northamptonshire, a schoolmaster, Owen Ragsdale, founded in 1591 Jesus Hospital, for a number of poor men variously put by different sources at twenty-four, twenty-six, and 'between twenty and thirty', who were, at any rate, provided with their clothing – top hats and coats with brass buttons – and ten shillings a week, and they also had a little garden each. They lived round a quadrangular courtyard entered by a heavy and rather forbidding stone gateway that reminds one of the workhouse in *Oliver Twist*, and indeed, although the archway is original much of the building round it is Victorian. I suppose the most interesting thing about this hospital is how the founder came to be so wealthy as to endow it. Not on the proceeds of school-teaching, one presumes, but I do not know the answer. His charity survives, anyway, and all he required in return was that his chest-tomb in the parish church should be well cared for.

At Stoneleigh, near Kenilworth, the so-called Old Almshouses were founded in 1594 by Sir Thomas Leigh and Alice, his wife. He was a Lord Mayor of London whose family had acquired the Cistercian abbey lands here after the Dissolution. Alice was married to Sir Robert Dudley later, and became Duchess of Dudley. The surviving almshouses, now called Dame Alice Leigh's, are five houses of red sandstone with prominent chimneys.

Cheriton Fitzpaine in Devon got its stone-built almshouses in the same year, endowed by the local Courtenays apparently in celebration of the victory over the Spanish Armada six years earlier. The building has huge chimneys, like buttresses, on the street side.

In London, Lady Dacre, recently widowed, founded the Emanuel Hospital in 1595 at Westminster. Her monument, with her effigy in alabaster, in company with that of her husband Gregory, Lord Dacre, is in Chelsea parish church, and survived Second World War bomb damage, but alas, her almshouses have long gone. They were rebuilt early in the eighteenth century in lavish style, round three sides of a courtyard with a lawn and shrubs. The main block had a central gabled frontispiece with an elaborately carved coat of arms in the tympanum and a clock and lantern above, with dormer windows in the dwellings flanking it. However, this building too has long been demolished, its place as a London charity, if not its actual site, having been taken by the less inspired United Westminster Almshouses.

Kirkthorpe in West Yorkshire got its Preston Hospital in 1595 also – a curious building with the dwellings round a dining hall which has their doors in it. The charity still exists, but at the time of writing the almshouses are scheduled for rebuilding.

Also still in existence is Jesus Hospital at Canterbury, founded in that city of long charitable tradition by Sir John Boys, again in 1595. It was built of brick on two storeys with gables, and accommodated seven poor men and four poor women, and among its rules was the provision that 'no domestic animal shall be kept by any Brother or Sister, save and except the Cat'.

The first ecclesiastical foundation of real importance after the Reformation was John Whitgift's Hospital at Croydon in 1596, after an Act of Parliament provided for its legal security – a wise precaution after the uncertainty of the earlier Tudor reigns. It was dedicated to the Holy Trinity and was the first almshouse founded by an archbishop since Chichele's at Higham Ferrers. It was built of red brick on two storeys round a quadrangle, with the chapel in one corner of the square and the kitchen in another, and was entered from the street by a gatehouse with the Primate's arms and mitre on the front in stone, and the words *Qui dat pavperi non indigebit* from *Proverbs* 28 – He that giveth unto the poor shall not lack. The archbishop had a private suite of rooms built in the hospital in which he occupied himself from time to time.

All the documents relating to the building contract survive, and we know that after the site was fenced round, the ground levelled, and footings made with flint, stones and other rubble, there was much trouble over the quality of the bricks. Samuel Finch, the vicar of Croydon, acted as Archbishop Whitgift's clerk of works, and was appointed governor of the hospital for life.

Women were soon allowed in, for the records show that on 2 October 1599, 'Thomas Elthon of the parish of Croydon, Blynde & of the Age of lxxj years: entred wth his aged wyfe'; and on the following day came 'Alice Dyble of the sayd parishe, Wydoe, and of the Age of lxxxviij years'. Alice Dyble's stay was not long, however, for she was recorded as 'Deceassed the xvijth day of November Anno Dm̄ 1600'. And in just over two years came the death of 'Our Moste Gratious Lorde John Whitgifte, Doctor of Dyvynitie, Archbishop of Canterburie, Primate & Metropolitan of all Englande Lorde of the moste Honorable privie Counsell, both to our late Queen Elizabeth, as also to our Dreade soveraigne Kyng James, that nowe ys'. The archbishop had also founded a free school which was closely connected with the hospital's affairs.

It is interesting to note that not only the inmates but also sometimes the wardens of hospitals were illiterate at this time, for one Robert Jenkins made his mark on a document of 1618, his name being written beside it by the schoolmaster, William Nicholson. It was a schoolmaster and not a warden, however, who was convicted of misappropriating hospital funds to the tune of £760 in 1812. There are several records of admonitions to inmates for quarrelling and fighting, slandering the foundation and its warden, and in one case for 'lewde and raylinge speaches both againste the Governors & all the whole bodie and members of the Hospitall'.

Some of the Whitgift Hospital's sources of revenue were reapportioned by the Charity Commissioners in the nineteenth century, and the buildings themselves have been threatened with demolition, but happily survive, among the few ancient buildings of note that modern Croydon can boast. The almshouses have lately been brought up to date to accommodate twenty-one residents in modern conditions, with bathrooms and central heating, and the conversion was carried out with minimal alteration to the outside appearance of the ancient buildings.

The Moyle almshouses at St German's, Cornwall

The old people here received visits from the Queen and the Archbishop of Canterbury nearly four hundred years after the first Elizabeth's archbishop founded the hospital.

Elizabeth I's chief minister was not to be left out of this sudden upsurge in charitable works. William Cecil's family ruled Stamford in Lincolnshire, that stylish town of mellow limestone, from the great Burghley House nearby, and in 1597, the year before his death, Lord Burghley founded the town's Burghley Hospital, on the site of the Hospital of St John and St Thomas founded in the twelfth century and suppressed at the Dissolution. Some of the Norman masonry remains in the Elizabethan buildings erected in St Martin's, with the fronts overlooking the River Welland. Stamford's prosperity came from the trade in woollen cloth, and its almshouses, usually founded by wealthy merchants, were often called 'Callis', from the Staple of Calais (an important market-place for traders in wool as well as leather, tin and lead).

Kent gained a hospital for twenty poor folk at Cobham in 1598, when William Brooke, tenth Lord Cobham, adapted a former chantry college for the purpose. The dwellings are built of ragstone on two storeys, and have delightful Gothic doors and latticed windows round three sides of a grassy quadrangle. The fourth side is occupied mainly by the original hall of the college, dating from the fourteenth century, which still has its original roof and fireplace, and the whole complex is serene and picturesque.

'Cast thy bread upon the waters' is inscribed over the entrance to the stone almshouses in a little square with a chapel at Barnwell, Northamptonshire. Although rebuilt in the nineteenth century, they were originally founded in 1601 by Nicholas Latham, the village parson, who also founded almshouses at Oundle in Northamptonshire ten years later. He was fondly imagined to have done all his charitable work out of his vicar's stipend, but in fact had an inheritance from his father.

Another adaptation took place in Rutland in the penultimate year of Elizabeth I, when the former palace of the bishops of Lincoln at Lyddington was made into a hospital for twelve men and two women by Thomas Cecil, Earl of Exeter and eldest son of the queen's chief minister, Lord Burghley. He endowed it with valuable lands and called it Jesus Hospital, but for some reason it has become popularly known as the 'Bede House'. It can never have been that.

The buildings, beside the village churchyard, are of the warm-coloured local ironstone, with mullioned windows and a steeply pitched roof. Lord Burghley divided one range into separate dwellings and made a cloister walk with a roof of stone tiles supported on massive oak posts. A stone staircase leads to the original hall on the upper floor, where the superb medieval ceiling of panelled oak has a carved cornice. Heraldic glass remains in the windows, and there are fine fireplaces, the one in the hall having over it the arms of Bishop Russell, who rebuilt the palace at the end of the fifteenth century. At one corner of the palace garden there is a little octagonal tower, through which the public pavement passes outside the garden wall, and this is thought to have been a watchtower. But all this is more to do

A corner of the quad at Cobham College, Kent

with medieval architecture than with almshouses, and sad to say, no aged poor live there any longer, the income from the foundation going instead to out-pensioners, who are still appointed by a descendant of Thomas Cecil.

Such peaceful places as Lyddington, where the old could spend their last years in relative comfort and quiet, seem to have inspired a certain amount of romanticism in the Elizabethans. Edmund Spenser, who was approaching the end of his own life in 1590, wrote and dedicated *The Faerie Queene* to Elizabeth, who was also approaching death, and visualized it in 'an holy Hospitall' where:

> . . . seven Bead-men, that had vowed all
> Their life to service of high heavens King,
> Did spend their daies in doing godly thing.
> Their gates to all were open evermore,
> That by the wearie way were traveiling;
> And one sate wayting ever them before,
> To call in commers-by that needy were and pore.

This affecting little picture was scarcely what was in the minds of many founders of almshouses in the latter part of the Tudor period. Many of them had amassed great fortunes from the proceeds of the Dissolution, or by shady deals, and if the saving of their souls was no longer the chief preoccupation of Protestant philanthropists in charitable works, there was at least a wish to be remembered for good works as a mitigation of their unscrupulous profiteering. The new Puritan ethic had no objection to the making of large profits as long as they were put to proper use, i.e. the greater glory of God.

Many almshouses or hospitals of ecclesiastical origin seemed almost like substitutes for the lost monasteries in the way they were built and run, and it is noticeable that, just as the abbots of the monasteries had become corrupt and lived in relative opulence instead of sharing the austere living conditions of their brethren, as the religious orders required them to do, so the masters of almshouses were increasingly provided with superior dwellings and private gardens which, in due course, were to lead to similar abuses of their founders' intentions.

It was probably around the time of Queen Elizabeth's death

that the Lord Howard de Walden, Earl of Suffolk and subsequently James I's Lord Treasurer, founded the fine Jacobean almshouses not far from his magnificent mansion at Audley End in Essex, on a former abbey property. They were built of brick round two courtyards, a hall, kitchen and chapel in one range recalling the medieval arrangement of hospitals, and separating one courtyard from the other. There were ten dwellings round each courtyard. These buildings are now the College of St Mark for retired clergymen.

How can we reconcile this apparent altruism with the earl's ruthless private capitalism, which led to accusations of embezzling a quarter of a million pounds of State money, and his wife's pension of a thousand pounds a year from Spain for divulging State secrets? Only on grounds of propitiation, surely. The Howards, after all, were Catholic.

The Tudors depended very heavily on private charity for the support of the poor. Elizabeth's Poor Laws were drawn up to buttress private charity in coping with the problem. But the extent to which compulsory poor rates and private charity between them *did* cope with the problem is relative. The rate for poor relief provided for financial assistance to such almshouses as might need it to carry on their work; yet in Newcastle alone, in 1596, thirty-two poor folk died of starvation in the streets.

Courtyard of the Charterhouse, London

4 Religious Foundations and the Rise of Capitalism

The first full year of James I's reign saw a harsh reinforcement of the Elizabethan laws for the punishment of 'rogues, vagabonds and sturdy beggars', which provided for fines of ten shillings against any members of the public who failed to apprehend vagrants. But the common horror of the idle able-bodied was balanced by a greater readiness on the part of wealthy Protestants to make endowments for the benefit of the poor in place of the casual alms and doles handed out by medieval Catholics.

By far the greatest portion of private charity in the Stuart period came from merchants and tradesmen. As Professor W. K. Jordan wrote in *Philanthropy in England*, 'the failure of a London merchant to settle some substantial and conspicuous charitable trust or gift was generally regarded as little short of shocking unless there had been a grievous wasting of the estate because of age, ill-health or commercial misfortune'. Philanthropists were encouraged to found and endow almshouses by a simplification of the legal procedure, a deed deposited in the Court of Chancery being sufficient, in place of the royal licence or Act of Parliament once required. It is reckoned that Britain as a whole had about 220 charities with resident accommodation in the seventeenth century, compared with only 55 in the sixteenth.

There was a distinct cessation of building during the Civil War and the period of the Commonwealth, but in spite of Calvinist strictures, it is evident that Protestants were just as generous to the needy as Catholics, and the Stuart period saw the building of some remarkable almshouses. Indeed, a study of the distribution of almshouses after the Reformation leads to the inescapable conclusion that the distribution corresponds exactly with the influence of the Church of England. That is to say, the farther north and west you go, the more sparse does almshouse-building become.

Professor R. H. Tawney wrote in *Religion and the Rise of Capitalism* 'the first forty years of the seventeenth century were prolific in the private charity which founded alms-houses and hospitals, and established funds to provide employment or to aid struggling tradesmen. The appeal was still to religion, which owed to poverty a kind of reverence'. However, the corresponding view commonly expressed, that *after* the Civil War the inclination towards charity was checked by a hardening of attitudes to social problems, is not really borne out by the evidence, as far as the foundation of almshouses is concerned. The later seventeenth century was, in this respect, just as prolific as the earlier period.

Among the earliest almshouses of the century were those at Bray and Lyford in Berkshire, however, where Catholics held sway in the Thames valley. Jesus Hospital at Bray was founded in 1609 by the will of William Goddard, who provided for the accommodation of forty poor persons, of whom six were to be freemen or women of the Fishmongers' Company (which still administers the foundation), and the rest parishioners of Bray over fifty years old. The brick-built hospital was completed in 1627, and consisted of chapel, kitchen and bakehouse as well as forty separate apartments with tall chimneys and dormer windows in the low roofs, round an attractive quadrangle. The dwellings have since been reduced in number and enlarged in size. The entrance front has a statue of the founder in a niche above the doorway, between mullioned, transomed and latticed windows. His tomb is in the parish church, with a rhyming autobiography on it.

In the following year the lord of the manor at Lyford, Oliver Ayscombe, founded some brick almshouses there, round three sides of a courtyard. Subsequently rebuilt, they are rather more humble than the homes at Bray.

Also in 1610, John Sedley built Trinity Hospital at Aylesford, Kent, for ten poor people. This consisted of a single row of gabled cottages, since restored and extended. And Alice Spencer, Countess of Derby, founded the modest almshouses bearing her name at Harefield, built of brick and with diagonal chimney-stacks; projecting wings formed an H-plan.

It was the year 1611 that claimed the first major architectural triumph of Stuart almshouses, though. Sir Thomas Sutton, who

Almshouses at Mapledurham, Oxfordshire – now converted into two cottages

had made his fortune from coal mining in the north of England, purchased for £13,000 a palace at Smithfield which had been built by the Howard family on the site of a Carthusian priory, and he founded there the hospital of King James, which has been commonly known ever since as the Charterhouse. It stood partly on the site of an old cemetery where possibly 20,000 dead were buried at the time of the Black Death, the priory having been founded there in 1371 as a memorial to them.

Sutton founded at the same time as his hospital an adjoining school for forty-four poor boys. The hospital itself was to accommodate eighty poor men, who were to be gentlemen fallen into poverty, old soldiers and sailors, merchants whose livelihood had been lost due to piracy or shipwreck, and former servants of the king's household. They must all be members of the Church of England. Their food and clothing was to be provided, attendance at chapel services was obligatory, and married inmates were forbidden to bring their wives. The master was to be a clerk in holy orders, and a corporation of distinguished governors controlled the foundation. These include today the Queen and the Archbishop of Canterbury. The buildings, which Sir Walter Besant called 'the most beautiful and most venerable monument of old London', were of three different periods and types when Sutton's work was finished, and formed a splendid complex of stone and brick, with fine gatehouses and courts, towers and oriel windows, the walls adorned with coats of arms, inscriptions and sundials. The Tudor great hall had a superb hammer-beam roof, and the Elizabethan great chamber had a gilded plaster ceiling and fine fireplace.

One of the brethren who spent their last years in these magnificent surroundings was the poet and dramatist Elkanah Settle, Dryden's rival, who lived in the Charterhouse from 1718 until his death six years later. Thackeray was one of several famous pupils of the Charterhouse School (Steele, Addison and Wesley were others) and described the place in his novel *The Newcomes* under the name 'Greyfriars'. Soon afterwards the school became Merchant Taylors' when Charterhouse School moved to Godalming. The buildings of the Charterhouse were badly damaged by bombing during the Second World War, but have been carefully restored to their former glory. The foundation has been affected, however, by a decline in its revenues owing to war damage, and fewer than half the original number of residents are accommodated there now. The chapel contains fine monuments by Stone, Flaxman and Chantrey to the founder; to Dr Raine, a headmaster of the school; and to Lord Ellenborough, the Lord Chief Justice who was educated at Charterhouse.

Sir Edward Montague built a smaller hospital close to the church at Weekley, Northamptonshire, in 1611. It no longer serves its former purpose of caring for seven poor men, but the buildings remain with their curious Jacobean entrance with obelisks, arms, a painted sundial and Latin inscriptions. Much more conventional were Lawrence Campe's brick almshouses of 1612 at Friern Barnet, also meant for seven (it will be noticed that the number thirteen had rather lost its magic by this time).

The almshouses of the same year at Chipping Campden in Gloucestershire are much better known. Founded by Sir Baptist Hicks, later·Viscount Campden, they form one long symmetrical range on a terrace facing the street, and were built in fine

Crisp's Almshouses at Marshfield, Gloucestershire

Cotswold style with eight gables and mullioned windows, the founder's coat of arms being in the centre. Sir Baptist provided for twelve old folk here. He was a financier and Lord Mayor of London, who did much other good work in this town, and his monument is in the parish church. His almshouses are accepted as a classic of Jacobean building, but I always find it disturbing that on the upper floor, the proportion of solid wall to window is so great.

They are, at any rate, much more generously conceived than the fifth Earl of Rutland's foundation at Bottesford, Leicestershire, also built in 1612, and very humble indeed, although he, Roger Manners, has one of the most magnificent of the famous monuments in the Rutland Chapel of the parish church.

In 1613, the actor-manager Edward Alleyn – Shakespeare's contemporary and rival (as an actor) – founded his College of God's Gift, now known as Dulwich College. It consisted of a school, chapel and almshouses, and the latter survive, the school having been rebuilt a little way to the south in the nineteenth century. Aubrey has it that Alleyn vowed to build the college when an apparition of the devil appeared to him during a performance of Shakespeare (more likely, perhaps, in Marlowe, as Dr Faustus was in Alleyn's repertoire!). Be that as it may, Alleyn had become wealthy, partly through an inheritance from his father and partly through his leading position in the theatre of the time and as King James's 'Master of the Bear Garden'; and when he died in 1625 he was buried in the college chapel.

The year 1613 was also the one in which John Lister founded his humble row of almshouses at Mapledurham in Oxfordshire. They were for six poor of the parish, and were built on one storey of chequer brick, with three pairs of doors with stone dressings, square two-light windows, and a steeply pitched slate roof (was it thatched once?). These almshouses were subsequently converted into two cottages.

New almshouses appeared at Greenwich, Castle Rising and at Clun between 1614 and 1618, all three of them founded by Henry Howard, Earl of Northampton. All were dedicated to the Holy Trinity and built on a similar quadrangular plan, with chapels projecting outwards from the square, and all three still exist, though alterations have taken place. The old ladies at Castle Rising in Norfolk still wear red cloaks and tall hats on ceremonial occasions. The hospital at Clun in Shropshire was for twelve poor men, but now there are ten dwellings for couples and six for single folk. They have formal gardens and vegetable plots, and still say a prayer in the chapel for the founder.

The corporate seal of Abbot's Hospital

The most impressive foundation of about that time, however, was at Hereford, where Sir Thomas Coningsby built his hospital for eleven poor old soldiers or sailors on the site of a former foundation of the Knights Hospitallers. The chapel, hall and apartments were built of stone round a rectangular courtyard on two storeys, one of the twelve dwellings being provided for the chaplain-master. Coningsby himself designed picturesque uniforms for the inmates – 'a fustian suit of ginger colour, of a soldier-like fashion, seemly laced, a soldier-like jerkin with half sleeves, and a square shirt, down half the thigh, with a moncado, or Spanish cap, a soldier-like sword, with a belt to wear as he goeth abroad, a cloake of red cloth lined with red baize'. According to legend, Nell Gwynn saw these almsmen in their elaborate costumes, and remembered them to advantage when Charles II founded the Royal Hospital at Chelsea; but there is no more truth in this than in most of the other tales about this wench. Coningsby, needless to say, was an old soldier himself, and the senior inmate was styled Corporal of Coningsby's Company of Old Servitors. The colourful company was seen marching through the streets of Hereford well into the present century.

Much more modest was the foundation of Sir Robert Napier at Dorchester in 1615. It provided for nine old men to receive free lodging and six shillings a week. The upper floor of the street-front was built over a stone cloister, with a gabled central entrance with a bell turret above it. Behind was a tiny courtyard. This quaint building, popularly known as 'Napper's Mite', has been threatened with demolition since the residents were housed elsewhere, but it survives, somewhat rebuilt, and is now a diminutive shopping precinct.

At Newland in the Forest of Dean, William Jones, a London haberdasher, founded in 1615 a long ten-bay row of Jacobean almshouses which run along one side of the village churchyard, and are administered by the Haberdashers' Company. And in the following year, Thomas Dutton built the row of gabled stone almshouses for poor old women at Northleach, on the Oxford road a long way from the church and shops, now having an almost medieval tumble-down look about them.

Sir John Kidderminster built a row of humble single-storey brick cottages at Langley Marish, near Slough, in 1617, and Elias Crisp built a row of eight gabled cottages in grey Cotswold limestone at Marshfield two years later, with little front gardens behind a high stone wall and a central clock tower and spire with a weather vane. But the most ambitious charities of 1619 were at Guildford and East Grinstead.

Trinity Hospital at Guildford was founded in that year by George Abbot, Archbishop of Canterbury, for both men and women, the twelve men being accommodated in a two-storey range on one side of the courtyard and the eight women opposite, the two ranges linked at one end by kitchen, dining hall and chapel, and at the other by the master's house and entrance gateway. Archbishop Abbot himself laid the foundation stone on 6 April, and his preface to the hospital's statutes declared: 'Forasmuch as every Christian man is bound, according to the measure of grace and mercy which he hath received from God, to render back again to his Eternal Father such tokens of grateful-

The courtyard at Guildford

ness and thankfulness as are in his power, and I, George Abbot, Archbishop of Canterbury, from the mere mercy of the Blessed God, besides the inward graces of his Holy Spirit, having been partaker of some earthly and worldly benefits more than most of my rank hath attained unto, I have held it agreeable with my duty to leave behind me to posterity some monument of my thankfulness to my Creator and some testimony of my faith in Christ Jesus, which, if it brings not forth some fruits to his glory, is to be held but as a dead and unprofitable faith; and therefore, my affection leading me to the town of Guildford wherein I was born and where my aged parents lived many years in good repute, I have thought upon erecting a Hospital there, which I have dedicated to the Blessed Trinity'.

The brethren and sisters were daily required to walk in procession to service in chapel in their uniforms of dark blue, the men also having silver badges. They were all to be over sixty years old and celibate, and either natives or long-term residents of Guildford.

The hospital was built of brick and modelled closely on Archbishop Whitgift's foundation at Croydon, but it has a more ambitious gatehouse with turrets at the angles of the tower-like building, and with a sundial and Abbot's arms above the doorway. There are chimneys of various shapes, and the windows have stone mullions and transoms, the whole having the classic Jacobean appearance in spite of the military-looking gatehouse. It stands at the top of the town's high street, across the road from the parish church in which its founder is buried, beneath an elaborate tomb bearing a lifelife if expressionless effigy. He is also represented in a formal and less lifelike manner on a memorial plate to his parents, Maurice and Alice Abbot, whose six sons also included a Bishop of Salisbury, a Lord Mayor of London, a Mayor of Guildford, and the first Master of George's foundation, his brother Richard.

The hospital or 'college' at East Grinstead was a little more homely in appearance. Built of sandstone round a most attractive quadrangle, one range was reserved for the use of the founder's family, and its ivy-covered walls with tall mullioned windows impart an architectural distinction uncommon in charitable enterprises. The hospital was founded by the will of Robert Sackville, Earl of Dorset, but not completed until ten years after his death in 1609, and his affairs being in a state of disorder, it was towards the end of the century before the finances of the hospital were finally settled. The earl's intentions were to accommodate twenty-one men and ten women, but this number had to be reduced before long.

As one enters the quadrangle from the entrance, the Dorset range is opposite, with the Sackville arms over the gabled entrance with a lantern above it. On the right, the centre of the range is occupied by the chapel, and on the left, the common kitchen and hall, and there is a tiled well-housing in the far left corner. The hall in the Sackville family's apartments eventually became the warden's quarters, and one of the nineteenth-century wardens here was John Mason Neale, the writer of many well-known hymns.

Like so many of the older almshouses, Sackville College is now a protected building, and its residents have been provided with modern facilities without alteration to the external appearance, with fifteen centrally-heated flats.

John Wynne and Richard Wyatt showed differing sympathies in their foundations at Baldock and Farncombe (near Godalming) respectively. The merchant Wynne provided his almshouses for twelve poor widows, intending his endowment to last 'to the worldes end' as an inscription on the front states optimistically, and under the six windows the date of the foundation is spelt out 'An No Do Mi Ni 1621'. Wyatt preferred men in his foundation of the following year, and housed them in plain brick dwellings with colossal and overwhelming chimney stacks at the back, but these provided arched inglenooks inside. The almshouses are administered by the Carpenters' Company, and are officially listed as 'Wyatt's Oyspital'.

Sir Anthony Ashley built the almshouses beside the church at Wimborne St Giles in Dorset in 1624. They are of red brick and stone on one storey except for a two-storey block in the centre, where there was originally a chapel above, and the foundation housed ten poor old people in single rooms. The Hext almshouses at Somerton in Somerset were put up in 1626 through the gift of Sir Edward Hext, and are a single row of one-storey dwellings built of the honey-coloured Ham Hill limestone, with oddly alternating square two-light windows and round-arched windows between the doorways, but otherwise very plain except for a little bell-turret on one end-gable.

Hext had been a Somerset Justice of the Peace much concerned about the problems of vagrancy in the Tudor period, and had corresponded with Lord Burghley on the need for urgent steps to curb the growth of crime arising from it in his county. He complained that the poor country people who had been robbed by vagabonds were now required to pay for feeding them when they were caught and locked up.

Inscription on the Hext Almshouses

Soon after Charles I replaced James on the throne, John Penrose, a mayor of Barnstaple, built the almshouses there which still bear his name. The front of the buildings in Litchdon Street is in characteristic Southwest style, with symmetrical low colonnades of granite pillars flanking the central gabled entrance porch. Behind this front is an attractive cobbled quadrangle, round which are twenty stone-built dwellings and a covered cloister walk, with dormer windows on the upper floor. The old pump is preserved in the middle of the quadrangle. These almshouses were not long built before the oak door to the board room received several bullet holes in the Civil War fighting, when the Royalists took the town but were ejected by the populace whose sympathies were with the Parliamentarians.

An arrowhead lodged in the front gate of some almshouses of 1627 at St Albans – a single-storey and very plain row of six – gave rise to fanciful explanations. Roger Pemberton of a prominent local family was the founder of this charity, and legend has it that the foundation was an act of atonement for Pemberton's accidental killing of an aged widow with an arrow when he was out hunting.

The charming little half-timbered Aubrey Hospital at Hereford was founded in 1630, for six poor women who were to be either spinsters or widows and over sixty years old. The tiny latticed windows in the gables have concave lozenges beneath them in the heavy oak framework. The founder was of the distinguished Aubrey family of Herefordshire from which the antiquary John Aubrey was descended, he being four years old at the time of its foundation.

Beaminster in Dorset acquired its humble almshouses by the churchyard in the same year, by the gift of Sir John Strode. They were for six poor people. Six were also accommodated at the attractive market town of Brackley in Northamptonshire, where in 1633 Sir Thomas Crewe built a single-storey range with dormers.

The years leading up to the Civil War saw some attractive almshouses being built, especially in the West Country. At Taunton, those founded by Robert Gray in 1635 were built in austere Jacobean style of brick on two storeys, with stone dressings. Coats of arms over the doorways are the only departure here from unadorned severity of style, but the foundation still exists and the town's gratitude to Robert Gray is seen on his monument in the parish church, with his painted effigy of life-size bearing the words:

Taunton bore him, London bred him,
Piety trained him, Virtue led him.

Quadrangle of the Penrose Almshouses, Barnstaple

Hugh Perry, who was born in Wotton-under-Edge in Gloucestershire and became Sheriff of London, left money to the mayor and aldermen of his native town for the almshouses in Church Street which housed six poor men and six poor women. Behind the gabled street front is a courtyard with a wooden gallery, on which is displayed the rules of the foundation, including the warning that those who fail to attend prayers in the little stone chapel shall be deemed to be unworthy of the charity.

Bullet holes in the board-room door at Barnstaple

Margaret Delabere's foundation at Chaddesley Corbett, Hereford and Worcestershire, and Sir George Croke's at Studley, Oxfordshire, still exist, dating from 1636 and 1637 respectively, and also in 1637 came the attractive almshouses at Moretonhampstead on the edge of Dartmoor. These latter were built of large squared blocks of moorland granite at the front, with a loggia facing the street, short granite columns supporting an arcade of fairly primitive appearance. Tiny mullioned windows on the upper floor shelter under the eaves, and the roof is thatched. No one seems to know who founded this charity, but it was undoubtedly someone who had made his money from the wool trade in the days when Moreton was a prosperous market town. The National Trust owns these buildings now.

Robert Hudson, subsequently made a baronet by Charles II, founded what was called, curiously for so late a date, a Maison Dieu in 1640 at Melton Mowbray, and it is still even now called the Bedehouse by some. It is close to the church, and has a stone front with three gables. It was founded for six old men who were to receive eighteen pence a week, and it was further endowed and extended later by a vicar of Melton, Rev. Storer. The buildings are scheduled for restoration at the time of writing.

Foundations at York, and at Chipping Norton and East Coker in Somerset were also completed in 1640. York's were built at Bootham by Sir Arthur Ingram, and have a massive central square tower of stone with a Norman arch brought here from the former priory of Holy Trinity at Micklegate. Henry Cornish built the gabled stone almshouses at Chipping Norton, and he is called 'gent' on the inscription. The almshouses at East Coker were also of stone, and the mellow golden limestone from the nearby quarries of Hamdon Hill gave these buildings a particular attractiveness. They were founded by Archdeacon Helyar, whose family long occupied Coker Court, and consist of twelve dwellings in a row, with mullioned windows and gables, and they share the approach to the church and manor house, making a fine grouping in this delightful stone village.

Although a few almshouses were built during the Civil War and its immediate aftermath, the period of political turmoil redounded badly on the poor, as always, the considerable private charitable activity of the first forty years of the century being interrupted until its slow revival after the Restoration. The Poor Laws of the time were making attempts to alleviate poverty by providing compulsory relief, setting the poor to work, apprenticing children to trades, and continuing to punish and reform the idle, but the aged poor and infirm still depended largely on charity, and in a time when wealthy men were defending their own security against revolutionary forces, it was not forthcoming. In years of great hardship for the labouring

*Entrance to the Perry Almshouses at Wotton-under-Edge,
Gloucestershire*

classes, when wages were depressed by government policy, one solution that began to be voiced was emigration to North America.

The Protestant incentive to philanthropy came partly, like the Reformation itself, from Continental influences. The Dutch, in particular, were setting civilized Europe an example in providing for their aged and infirm poor. The hospital for lame and decrepit soldiers founded in Amsterdam in 1587 was to excite the admiration of the diarist John Evelyn as 'one of the worthiest things that I think the world can show of that nature'. Sir William Temple, the English ambassador to the Netherlands, observed: 'Charity seems to be very National among them, though it be regulated by Orders of the Countrey, and not usually moved by the common Objects of Compassion'. He was especially impressed by an almshouse for aged seamen at Enkhuizen. Prominent citizens – both men and women – served on the governing committees of these almshouses, and as was the custom in seventeenth-century Holland, had their group portraits painted for their board rooms. Some of the best of these pictures were done at Haarlem by Frans Hals, who was himself reduced to living on charity in his old age.

William Carr, the English consul in Amsterdam, wrote that acts of charity there were 'so extraordinary that they surpass all other cities in the world, for they are daily and hourly giving to the poor'. Officers of the city's almshouses made house-to-house collections twice a week, regularly raising large sums, and Charles II remarked, when the French invaded the United Provinces in 1672, that God would preserve Amsterdam 'if only for the great charity they have for the poor'.

Reports of these and other Englishmen of the great and good works done by the Calvinist Dutch without any promise of heavenly reward must have influenced English Protestants emerging from the Reformation with a somewhat confused moral philosophy, and made the Tudor period only a temporary lull in the English inclination to charitable works.

Stafford acquired a 'college' for twenty-four old folk in 1645, by the gift of Sir Martin Noel, the central chapel flanked by six stone dwellings on either side, with an open court. Four years later came the execution of Charles I, and a gap of eight years before we find another foundation of note – that of Sir William

The almshouses at Moretonhampstead, Devon

Drake at Amersham, a town with a strong Protestant background and Cromwellian sympathies. This is a modest but attractive composition of single-storey brick dwellings round three sides of a small court, with a wall and gateway closing the fourth side to the street. The Drake family were lords of the manor of Amersham for centuries, and their monuments in the church, including Sir William's, form an unusually rich collection.

An eccentric-looking almshouse at Denton, Lincolnshire, should be mentioned. Built in 1653 in the former park of the Welby lords of the manor, it is a building of mellow brown ironstone with extraordinary Dutch gables, round windows, and dressings of grey stone, with huge chimney stacks.

The twenty years from 1646 saw the development of almshouses at Barnstaple by three of the town's citizens on the site of an earlier foundation in Church Lane. Thomas Harris provided the first almshouse here, and this was added to in 1656 by Elizabeth Paige, wife of a mayor of the town, when four more houses were built alongside. Then in 1665 Thomas and Alice Horwood founded eight further almshouses, Alice having

Courtyard of the Drake Almshouses, Amersham

REPAIRED IMPROVED
AND FURTHER
ENDOWED BY
BENJAMIN GOODWIN ESQ
FORMERLY OF
SAINT EDMONDS BURY
AND MANY YEARS
AN INHABITANT
OF THIS PARISH
ANNO 1767.

*The Meggs' Almshouses at
West Ham in the
nineteenth century*

already provided the town with a school for twenty poor girls. Eventually the thirteen houses were reduced to twelve and then to nine, to provide better accommodation, but they survive with a little cobbled court in the town centre.

In Yorkshire, 1657 saw the appearance of the twelve single-storey and humble almshouses in the delightful village of Thornton-le-Dale. Each has a door and one window at the front. They were founded, together with the village's grammar school, by Lady Lumley, whose family were lords of the manor of Scarborough.

Canterbury also got a new almshouse in 1657 with John and Ann Smith's row of eight single-storey cottages, and the year before Charles II came to the throne, James Smith built a row of eight at Maidenhead, which still exists in the care of the Salters' Company – single-storey brick dwellings with gabled dormers.

At West Ham in London, William Meggs built and endowed a two-storey row of brick almshouses in 1658, with a central pediment and coat of arms, and these were improved and further endowed a century afterwards by Benjamin Goodwin.

In a more settled nation, the requirements of a civilized state again took some precedence in the minds of leading men, and the building of almshouses got a distinct lift after the Restoration. Dr Johnson was to say in due course that 'a decent provision for the poor is the true test of civilization'. We might retort to Johnson's ghost that the only true test of civilization is that there should not *be* any poor! But if this conception was beyond the capacity of seventeenth- and eighteenth-century thinkers, at least provision for the poor was a growing concern of responsible people, though private charity still did more than the State.

When the Great Plague broke out in London in 1664, it was alleged by some to have originated in the Drapers' Company almshouses, which had been founded around 1524, in the parish of St Olave. Between 70,000 and 100,000 Londoners are believed to have died in the epidemic, but modern historians absolve the almshouses of responsibility for the outbreak, and ascribe its origin to a point further west. Did the suspicion originate in an association of ideas – the old link between almshouses and leprosy? At any rate, the accused building was destroyed in the Great Fire soon afterwards.

In 1661, Pembridge in Hereford and Worcestershire got its Duppa Almshouses, originally six cottages now reduced to four. Lewisham, Wokingham, Gamlingay, Corsham, Bromley and Hereford also got important new charities in the first decade after the Restoration. Of these the most distinguished architecturally are those at Wokingham, Bromley and Corsham.

The Fauconberg Hospital at Coxwold, North Yorkshire

The Henry Lucas Hospital at Wokingham, Berkshire, was founded in 1665 and is a splendid Stuart building of brick, south of the town. It has a long front with projecting wings, all of two storeys, and a pediment with coat of arms in the centre and a cupola above. A walled garden is in front and the whole composition seems very advanced for the time.

Bromley College in Kent was founded by John Warner, Bishop of Rochester, in 1666, for the widows of clergymen who had been both 'orthodoxe and loyall', and is another mature piece of building design of the period. The architect was Richard Ryder, and he provided exceptionally spacious accommodation for the ladies, each of whom had two ground-floor rooms and a kitchen, and two bedrooms upstairs, not to mention a resident servant each. The college is built of brick and has projecting wings flanking the long front, in the centre of which is a Portland stone frontispiece with a curved pediment above the entrance arch, with Bishop Warner's arms on an escutcheon.

By comparison with these advanced Caroline almshouses on the grand scale, the Hungerford almshouses at Corsham in Wiltshire seem positively medieval, but they are undeniably attractive. Founded by Dame Margaret Hungerford in 1668, they were intended for six destitute old women, and consist of L-shaped stone buildings with much Gothic detail and such flamboyant arms and inscriptions that one suspects a throw-back to the days when founders of charities were seeking self-glorification.

The north range of the buildings were the almshouses and the west range a school, and as well as the elaborately carved Hungerford arms above both entrances, there are identical inscriptions as follows:

This Free School and Almshouse was founded and endowed by Margaret Lady Hungerford, relict of Sir Edward Hungerford, Kt., of the Honourable Order of the Bath, daughter and co-heire of William Halliday, Alderman of London, and Susan his wife, daughter of Sir Henry Row, Knight, and Alderman and Lord Mayor of London.

The buildings have almost as many gables as Corsham Court, the Hungerfords' home, and above the former school range there is a tall bell turret. The school became the master's house, but the original schoolroom remains intact, complete with the master's pulpit chair.

Sir William Morton, one of the king's justices in the Court of Common Pleas, founded an almshouse at Kidlington, Oxfordshire, in 1671, in memory of his wife Ann, which had the names of his family inscribed on lintels over the windows – 'Mr. William's Roome', 'Madam Ann's Roome', etc. And at Worlaby in Lincolnshire Lord Bellasis built his almshouses for four poor widows and provided for each of them a new blue gown every year, and three pounds ten shillings and coal for their fires.

A year later Sir John Tregonwell founded his almshouses at

Milton Abbas in Dorset for six poor widows, but these were demolished about a century afterwards, along with the rest of the old town, by the ruthless Earl of Dorchester, and eventually rebuilt in his model village, preserving not only the original endowment, but parts of the original building too. Was the founder here that same John Tregonwell who had survived a fall from the top of the church tower when he was a five-year-old boy, saved by his infant's clothing acting as a parachute? Some of the later residents of the old village might have wished that young Joseph Damer, the future earl, had fallen off it when *he* was five!

Elizabeth Viscountess Lumley, who founded a row of single-storey almshouses at Shoreditch in 1672, was the same lady who was responsible for the almshouses at Thornton-le-Dale in Yorkshire, fifteen years earlier. The London buildings were brick cottages, but they were demolished in 1822. Gabriel Richards founded the almshouses which still bear his name at Goodnestone in Kent some time before 1672, small and of red brick, and his monument in the church calls them, in Greek, the 'poor-house'.

Kirkleatham in Cleveland was the site in 1676 of a magnificent foundation by Sir Marwood William Turner, a wool draper and Lord Mayor of London, who had been a leading figure in the rebuilding of the capital after the Great Fire of 1666. The whole hospital at Kirkleatham was more or less rebuilt by his great-nephew Cholmley Turner in 1742, and is an imposing composition of brick and rugged northern stonework, with a particularly fine chapel and a school attached. The almshouses were for ten men and ten women, and the school for ten boys and ten girls. Fine wrought-iron gates lead into the courtyard, and a superb iron balustrade links the side galleries in the chapel. There is a bust of the founder over the doorway. The extraordinary Turner mausoleum by Gibbs is attached to the parish church.

Sir William Turner's generous foundation (it was in Yorkshire's North Riding when he built it) was the only serious rival to the Royal Hospitals at Chelsea and Greenwich among those built in the latter half of the seventeenth century. Sir William did not want his residents to consider themselves receivers of charity, but as his 'guests'. They lived in the ranges for 'masters' and

'mistresses' on the north and south sides of the courtyard, with the range linking them occupied by the chapel and school. Fine statues of an old man and woman are in niches, whilst in the middle of the courtyard stands a statue of Justice. The present occupants of Kirkleatham live in cottages with their own garden plots.

A rather less ambitious foundation was John Sayer's at Berkhamsted, Hertfordshire, in 1681, a row of six brick single-storey cottages for poor widows, with the provision every other Christmas of a cloth gown for each. These almshouses have subsequently been reduced to four dwellings.

The Vernon family, lords of the manor of Sudbury in Derby-shire, were among the early exponents of building almshouses in model villages, their almshouses going up in 1678. They set the

Almshouses founded by Lady Lumley at Shoreditch. They were demolished in 1822

example for such as the Duke of Bedford at Woburn and Baron Ferdinand de Rothschild at Waddesdon in Buckinghamshire.

Sir Christopher Wren's name first appears in connection with the subject of almshouses around this time. He is sometimes said to have designed the brick almshouses at Farley, Wiltshire, founded by Sir Stephen Fox in 1681, six dwellings of brick, for both men and women, in a single row of two storeys, with the warden's house in the middle, facing the churchyard gates. Wren's name has also been suggested in connection with the design of Kirkleatham Hospital. It seems unlikely, to say the least, that he had anything to do with these, but his connection with the Collegium or Matrons' College at Salisbury is more certain and more obvious. It stands just inside the north gate to the cathedral close, and was founded in 1682 for ten clergymen's

The imposing entrance of the Royal Hospital, Chelsea

widows by the bishop, Seth Ward, who was an old friend of
Wren's. This is a long building of exceptional stylishness behind
a low brick wall, with projecting wings having circular windows
in the dormers, a cornice, central pediment and octagonal
lantern, diagonal chimney-stacks, and garlanded coat of arms. It
was built in English bond brickwork at a time when Flemish
bond was coming into favour generally. The first elderly women
who moved into it must have felt they were living in a palace
after the humble rectories they came from.

Seth Ward also founded the almshouses at Buntingford,
Hertfordshire, in 1684, though his less illustrious architect there
produced a more conventional building in the classical style, still
stately enough for a country village, to be sure, with eight
dwellings for four men and four women round three sides of a
courtyard facing the village street. The bishop was educated at
Buntingford grammar school, having been born at Aspenden,
nearby, and he became Professor of Astronomy at Oxford
before his high office in the Church of England.

He died in 1689, in poverty of a sort himself, for Aubrey tells us that 'The black malice of the Deane of Sarum – he printed sarcasticall Pamphletts against him – was the cause of his disturbd spirit, wherby at length, he quite lost his memorie. For about a moneth before he dyed he tooke very little Sustenance, but lived on the Stock, and died a Skeleton'.

At Croston, Lancashire, there was no hint in the almshouses built there that a whole new architectural style was about to envelop charity homes. A very basic row of one-storey cottages, with a roof of graded stone tiles increasing in size from ridge to eaves, proclaims itself 'Erected by Henry and Isabel Croston An Do 1692'.

Seth Ward's friend Wren, meanwhile, the King's Surveyor, was preoccupied with an altogether more ambitious project. In 1670, Louis XIV had founded the Hôtel des Invalides in Paris for no less than 7,000 disabled soldiers. The vast building took five years to complete (the church was finished much later), and has since been regarded as one of the finest architectural achievements in Paris. The Merry Monarch decided to emulate the Sun King, and got Wren to design what came to be the Royal Hospital, Chelsea. Sir Stephen Fox, founder of the almshouses at Farley, played a leading role in its inception as Paymaster

Oak Apple Day parade in the courtyard at Chelsea

General, providing large Army funds and undertaking responsibility for the hospital's administration. Wren chose the site,
facing the Thames, and designed a brick building with stone
dressings, with three ranges round a courtyard. The main range
facing the river contains the hall and chapel on either side of a
vestibule, fronted by a classical portico of Doric columns, with a
loggia on either side and a cupola above. The side ranges are of
four floors in plain unadorned style, each divided up into
separate apartments for the pensioners. In the centre of the
courtyard is one of London's finest open-air statues, of the
founder, Charles II, in Roman costume. It is by Grinling
Gibbons, in bronze, and was set up here probably in the year of
the hospital's completion, in 1692.

The hospital was never intended to be on the vast scale of its
Paris inspiration, and when it was opened, nearly five hundred
old soldiers moved in. They are still selected from army veterans,
and must be sixty-five or over and men of good character. The
pensioners' uniforms of scarlet frock-coats and three-cornered
cocked hats, with dark blue winter overcoats, make them instantly recognizable, and date in fact from the dress of
Marlborough's soldiers twenty years after Charles II's death.
They parade here annually on Oak Apple Day (29 May), the
anniversary of their founder's restoration to the throne.

'Here,' wrote Defoe, 'is the noblest building, and the best
foundation of its kind in the world. . . . If we must except the
hospital called Des Invalids at Paris, it must be only that the
number is greater there, but I pretend to say that the economy of
the invalids there, is not to compare with this at Chelsea; and as
for the provisions, the lodging and attendance given, Chelsea
infinitely exceeds that at Paris.'

Despite this great royal example to others, however, not
everyone was entirely sold on the wisdom of spending their
money on such charity. Hugh Squier, for instance, a rich merchant of South Molton, Devon, saw more virtues in arithmetic,
and founding a school there to teach it, delivered himself of the
opinion that arithmetic is as necessary as 'salt unto our meat'.
Therefore, he wrote, 'whyles others build Almshouses to relieve
the poor, I do design to prevent them from ever being poor, and
instead of living in others Almeshouses, that some of these may
in tyme build Almshouses for others to live in'.

Trinity Hospital in London's Mile End Road

Up in Newcastle upon Tyne, nevertheless, whilst the Chelsea Hospital was only being begun in London, Holy Jesus Hospital had been built and endowed by the town's corporation in very different style, though also of brick, with a long arcade at the front and Dutch end gables. And before Chelsea's completion, new almshouses were built at Blandford Forum, Froxfield, Quainton and Bristol, among other places. Bristol's were founded by the philanthropist Edward Colston, this building being of two storeys round three sides of a courtyard – the prevailing fashion – with a hipped roof and pantiles. Colston's various charitable works in Bristol were motivated largely by his fanatical High-Anglicanism and his horror of Dissent.

Most impressive of these foundations is that at Froxfield, Wiltshire. The hospital was founded by Sarah, Dowager Duchess of Somerset, in 1686, for the widows of clergymen, and was instantly an almshouse of very considerable size, but it was enlarged a hundred years later, and indeed virtually doubled in size, with accommodation for twenty clergymen and thirty widows. The buildings enclosed a large oblong quadrangle, in the middle of which is a stone-built chapel, but the almshouses are built of brick, the earlier part with stone mullions in the windows, the later with wooden windows, on either side of a stone gateway.

Chipping's aged poor, in Lancashire, benefited in 1684 from the will of John Brabin, a cloth dyer, who left money for the building of the almshouses and school there, the two-storey almshouses being of plain and rugged northern style with rubble-stone walls and stone-tiled roofs. At Cossall, Nottinghamshire, the Willoughby Hospital of 1685 is a brick group, with a saddleback roof in the middle, and though hardly in the latest fashion of the time, attractive for all that.

The Royal Hospital for old soldiers at Chelsea had hardly opened its doors before the new king, William III, with some prompting, apparently, from the queen, decided to rebuild an unfinished royal palace at Greenwich as a home for old and disabled sailors. Although several architects contributed to the

The classical front of Morden College, Blackheath

Royal Naval Hospital over the following decades, including Hawksmoor and Vanbrugh, the chief designer was again Sir Christopher Wren, who this time composed a masterpiece of baroque architecture, once again facing the Thames across an open courtyard. But although the hospital housed over 2,000 naval pensioners after the Napoleonic Wars, the hospital ceased its charitable function in 1869, and four years later became the Royal Naval College.

Merchant seamen, meanwhile, were provided for at Bristol by the two-storey rendered and pantiled buildings round a pleasant courtyard, founded in 1696 by the Company of Merchant Adventurers, and now known as Merchants' Almshouses. In London, Trinity Hospital served a similar purpose, being founded about the same time by the Corporation of Trinity House for twenty-eight 'decay'd masters and commanders of ships or ye widows of such'. This place is said to have been originally designed by Wren, and consisted of two rows of brick dwellings along the sides of a long courtyard with trees and a statue, and with a detached chapel at one end, opposite the entrance gates from Mile End Road. Both these hospitals were affected by the Second World War, London's being badly damaged by bombing. Trinity Hospital, restored in the late 1950s, is still a peaceful oasis in the arid east London conglomeration, its street front ornamented with model galleons. The statue is no longer in the courtyard, and the chapel now serves as a welfare centre.

Another hospital attributed to Wren was Morden College at Blackheath, founded by Sir John Morden for 'decayed Turkey merchants' in 1695. This is a fine classical building in landscaped grounds, and is built of brick with stone dressings, round a large quadrangle. The central range has a pediment with statues of the founder and his wife in niches, and a cupola above. The attribution to Wren is based on the facts that the builder was Edward Strong, who worked with Wren frequently, and that Sir John Morden was associated with Wren on the Greenwich Hospital Commission. This attractive building is certainly worthy of the great architect.

A sort of rural version of this stately late Stuart style was built in 1697 at Ampthill in Bedfordshire by John Crosse, and named Oxford Hospital. It was for former college servants of Oxford.

The central bay with its pediment and cupola above was designed as the chapel in this case. The foundation survives as John Crosse's Charity.

At Maidstone in 1700, Sir John Banks founded his six almshouses and built them in brick, and at Bradford-on-Avon in Wiltshire John Hall built the Kingston almshouses for four poor men, in stone, both single rows in styles characteristic of the time; the building at Bradford-on-Avon being fronted by a low stone wall with stone urns, and the founder's coat of arms is in the centre; whilst at Newcastle-on-Tyne in 1701 the Keelmen's Hospital was built of brick round a quadrangle, close to the river and well outside the town at that time. The keelmen paid for it themselves.

At Worcester in 1702, the year of Queen Anne's accession, the Berkeley Hospital was built, founded by Robert Berkeley, renewing an earlier foundation by his grandfather for twelve poor men. The street front consists of two blocks of brick with stone dressings and tall windows, on two storeys, and between them an iron gateway which leads into a rectangular tree-lined courtyard with the single-storey almshouses on either side and the chapel at the end, much like the Trinity Hospital of a few years before in London. Berkeley was a diplomat in Holland, and the buildings show clear Dutch influence. The founder's statue is in a niche over the pedimented door of the chapel, and each door of the almshouses has a triangular tympanum with a shield bearing the founder's arms. Self-exaltation could scarcely go further in such simple domestic architecture.

What a difference at Great Yarmouth, where the Fishermen's Hospital of the same year was founded by the town's corporation, and has a figure of Charity in the courtyard, which is surrounded on three sides by gabled single-storey dwellings of brick, with returning projections on the fourth side ending in Dutch gables and forming the entrance. The dwellings have latticed windows, directly above which are dormers in the roofs, and above the doorway opposite the entrance is a pediment with a ship in relief, beneath a lantern. This building gives the impression of a homely community as opposed to the more imposing formality of the time in the cities.

By the market place in Abbots Bromley in Staffordshire are the Bagot Almshouses, built in brick in 1705 on two storeys with a

Twitty's Almshouses of 1707 at Abingdon

central curly pediment; while Abingdon added to its existing
almshouses round the churchyard when Charles Twitty founded
in 1707 a home for three poor old men and three poor old
women, and left money 'of his pious inclination' for maintaining
them in 'Meate, Drinke and Apparel and all other Necessaryes of
life'. The single-storey range has a central pediment and a square
lantern above it with a ball finial surmounted by a weather
vane.

Two years after this, Abel Collins built his almshouses in Friar
Lane at Nottingham. Sir Nikolaus Pevsner described this building as 'one of the best almshouses of its date in England', and it
presented a well proportioned and unfussy symmetry to the
street, with a central arched entrance to the quadrangle, round
which were built twenty two-storey houses, each with living
room and larder on the ground floor and bedroom upstairs. A
sundial, arms and inscription are carved over the doorways, and
tall chimney-stacks enhance the perfect symmetry of the buildings. Nottingham has scarcely received its due in this book so

far, for it is actually among the leading towns of England in its promotion of charitable foundations, but it is a city which has undergone a great deal of redevelopment since the Industrial Revolution, and few of the older foundations remain in anything like their original form.

At Paul, Cornwall, a tomb in the church has an inscription in the old Cornish language which, translated, reads:

> Eternal life be his whose loving care
> Gave Paul an almshouse and the church repair.

The tomb is that of Captain Stephen Hutchins, who died in 1709 and left money for the Hutchens almshouses beside the churchyard, plain with slabs of granite framing the windows, and called at one time the Gift House. Also in Cornwall are the eighteenth-century Rashleigh Almshouses, on the road west from Fowey to Par, a pretty row of cottages rebuilt as recently as 1972.

It was in the last years of Queen Anne that Sir Robert Geffrye's almshouses were built for the Ironmongers' Company at Shoreditch. Sir Robert had been master of the company and a Lord Mayor of London. There were three ranges of houses round a very spacious courtyard, the fourth side enclosed by low walls. The chapel was in the centre of the main range with a statue of the founder in a niche over the doorway, and with a bell turret on the roof. The almshouses were beyond the main area of Shoreditch when they were built, but gradually became swamped by industrial development. In 1912, the foundation was moved to Mottingham, Kent (which is ironically itself now well inside Greater London), in new premises modelled on Morden College at Blackheath. Meanwhile, the former alms-houses at Shoreditch became the Geffrye Museum, devoted to furniture and woodwork. The old buildings were saved from demolition by the National Trust, which raised £24,000, the largest portion of which came from the London County Council. The ghost of 'Sr Rob. Geffryes, Knt., Alderman and Ironmonger' must, we may be sure, have looked on this development with some unease, his charity having been deprived of both his name and his building.

At Ravenstone, on the Leicestershire coalfield, Rebecca Wilkins founded a hospital in 1711 in memory of her son. This

The Wilkins almshouses at Ravenstone, Leicestershire

was an ambitious composition which was not finally completed until the end of the century, but happily it survives intact. Built of mellow brick round a quadrangle, with a chapel and a master's house flanking the main range, it is one of those large formal buildings that are always slightly surprising in small rural communities or even, in this case, industrial villages, though it has to be added that the grassy courtyard now has a run-down look and is untidily cluttered with washing lines and privies.

We know of a lost opportunity at Humberston, on the coast near Grimsby, for Robert Adam, no less, designed almshouses for Matthew Humberston's foundation, but his plans were not carried out, though the founder's monument in the church tells us that he left money for rebuilding the church, building and endowing a school as well as the almshouses, increasing the vicar's stipend, and erecting his own monument. Perhaps he was too optimistic as to how far his fortune, made from 'places of Trust and profit in the Custom house' would go. The almshouses were built, but on much less ambitious lines.

So ended the Stuart period which, whatever its other failings, had responded to the needs of the poor and aged in positive and even magnificent fashion, setting standards of social caring in England which we can perhaps liken to private generosity today in response to famine and disaster in Third World countries.

5 Private Charity in a Secular Century

After the Stuart period, private charity declined somewhat as the State assumed increasing if reluctant responsibility for the poor. Nearly a fifth of the population was receiving some form of poor relief in the early eighteenth century. The Poor Law which empowered each parish in the land to raise taxes for the relief of the impotent poor, including the building of poorhouses, and to keep the able-bodied at continual labour, was reinforced by increasingly savage laws against theft – one of the consequences of widespread poverty. The time was approaching when the penalty for stealing a loaf of bread to ward off starvation was death by hanging, and the horrors of the workhouse system loomed on the horizon.

Maybe as the population of paupers grew ever greater, and the gap between rich and poor widened, those rich who did not feel compelled to help the poor from religious motives – for this was an irreligious age – were unable to see any practical virtue in individual action in the face of such an immense problem. Indeed, as Henry Fielding wrote: 'So very useless, indeed, is this heavy tax, and so wretched its disposition, that it is a question whether the Poor or the Rich are more dissatisfied . . . since the plunder of one serves so little to the real advantage of the other'.

Certainly there was a growing public conviction that it was in society's interests to keep the poor hungry to make them industrious, and the workhouse was the logical tool of the doctrine that any handout to the genuinely poor should be accompanied by penalties. One of the arguments against building large numbers of houses for the growing population of London was that a huge influx of poor people living in insanitary conditions would endanger the delicate health of the queen!

Many aged poor continued to benefit, however, from the

*The Herbert Almshouses at Preston-upon-the-Weald-Moors,
Shropshire*

generosity of a few who had no such misgivings, and there is
some reason to think that charity was moving north, possibly
with the spreading influence of the Church of England, though
the clergy's own contribution to poor relief was pathetic and,
since they were constantly exhorting their congregations to acts
of charity, hypocritical as well.

The first good example in the reign of George I was set by the
Duke of Beaufort at Great Badminton, Avon, where the ducal
arms adorn three pediments on the stone almshouses built in the
model village around 1714. The uniform stone and gabled style
of all building in the Cotswolds sometimes makes almshouses
more difficult to recognize than in other areas, and Great
Badminton's are no exception. The village post office looks more
like an almshouse than the real ones.

It could be argued, of course, that such establishments were
raised by conscience, since they were intended for estate servants
who had not enough money to live on when they retired. But that
could hardly apply to the next foundation we notice. It was built

at Preston-upon-the-Weald-Moors, an out-of-the-way village on a marshy windswept plain in Shropshire, in 1716, at the behest of Lady Katherine Herbert, widow of Lord Herbert of Chirbury. She left £6,000 for the building and endowment of an almshouse for twelve poor women and twelve poor girls, the latter to be taught reading, writing and sewing. Legend has it that Lady Herbert was moved to this act of charity by her gratitude for being saved from death in the Alps by St Bernard dogs.

At any rate, the buildings were erected and further endowed by other members of her family, and resulted in what Sir Nikolaus Pevsner has called 'a most spectacular example of Georgian almshouse architecture'. They are of red brick with stone dressings, and in the classic form of buildings enclosing three sides of a courtyard, but on the grand scale. Two lodges at the roadside flank the gateway to an attractive avenue of lime trees leading to the courtyard, which is protected by splendid wrought-iron gates. The hall faces the gates in the centre of the range across the courtyard, with a square lantern and clock on its roof, which has a parapet. The wings with arcades enclose the courtyard on either side and end in elegantly curved extensions that almost seem like a welcoming embrace offered to the approaching visitor. There is no question of the superb stylishness of this almshouse in such an unlikely setting, and the only temptation to doubt is to wonder whether too much of the available money was spent on fine architecture and not enough on the care of the poor. The building was not cheap, and even the gates would grace a royal palace.

Later gifts enabled the number of women taken in to be increased to twenty, however, and girls were taken in at the age of seven and trained until they were sixteen in 'whatsoever could make them useful servants'. Ay, there's the rub. They could be made useful to the rich and thus bring them a return on their investments. But it is too easy to impute less than noble motives to philanthropists of any age, and at least these fortunate girls were housed, fed, clothed and educated, and given five pounds-worth of clothing when they left. Girls are no longer taken in, of course, and both wings are nowadays occupied by elderly women and a few couples, all of whom enjoy the modern luxuries of private bathrooms and central heating.

Whilst the Herbert almshouse – or the Preston Trust Home as
it is now called – was being built in Shropshire, a similarly grand
conception was taking shape in Yorkshire, and in an equally
unlikely place – the small village of Linton in Wharfedale.
Completed at about the same time, in 1721, this establishment
was the foundation of Richard Fountaine, the lord of the manor,
who built his hospital for six poor women on the other side of
the village green from his own home, Linton Hall. Fountaine
was, among other things, a timber merchant, with a special
interest in the supply of coffins, apparently, for he had charge of
disposal of the dead in London at the time of the Great Plague in
1664. He was also timber merchant to Sir John Vanbrugh, so the
latter has naturally been suggested as the designer of Fountaine's
Hospital. It seems more incongruous than the Preston building,
but again undeniably impressive as charity architecture. Here
the small entrance court is fronted by a low wall, presumably an
afterthought built to protect it when the roadway was made
round the village green. Behind this rises the main façade of
stone, with a central domed tower, behind which is the chapel,
and this range is flanked by short projecting wings with pediments. The founder's uncompromising sex discrimination is no

Sir Thomas Hanmer's almshouses at Mildenhall, Suffolk

longer upheld, for men have an equal right to be poor and infirm, and they are allowed in too.

The so-called Rector's Almshouses of the same time at Sunderland can hardly compete in style, but they served the same compassionate purpose, as did the 1722 foundation at Highgate in London, the modest Woolaston-Paunceforth Almshouses.

Penny's Hospital at Lancaster rejected the grand approach in 1720, favouring instead two ranges of single-storey cottages facing each other across a narrow cobbled courtyard, at the end of which was a chapel, opposite the gabled entrance wall with an iron gate in it. Twelve poor people were provided for here. Alongside the churchyard at Mildenhall, Suffolk, Sir Thomas Hanmer built a simple row of houses in 1723, for four poor widows of the parish, and at Hawkhurst, Kent, brick almshouses adjoined a school, both being 'Given by Sir Thomas Dunk Kt. 1723'.

Nor were all the wealthy of Oxfordshire inclined to jump on the architectural bandwagon set in motion by Charles II's Royal Hospital at Chelsea forty years earlier. Goring Heath and Witney in that county acquired new almshouses in 1724, Witney's being provided for six widows of the town's blanket makers. These were entirely rebuilt in 1868. At Goring Heath, however, Henry Allnatt, a Lord Mayor of London, desired some distinction in design for the almshouses he founded, and his architect followed the classic model to produce a building round three sides of a courtyard, with a low wall on the entrance side as at Linton. Here there were eight dwellings on one storey, with a chapel in the centre and a cupola above. The bell-shaped gable in the centre and the end gables of the wings are decorated with acorn finials.

Frolesworth in Leicestershire is another of those unknown country villages that seem surprising settings for ambitious architecture for charitable purposes, but John Smith, Lord Chief Baron of the Exchequer in Scotland, founded an almshouse here in 1725, in the place of his birth, and it was again designed in contemporary fashion to enclose three sides of a square. This foundation has been considerably extended since that time, and is now largely a Victorian building, but an inscription over the porch, with a quotation from Alexander Pope, recalls one of the more illustrious of the world's John Smiths:

Who built this Almshouse neat, but void of state,
Where Age and Want sit smiling at the gate.

They were not so smiling at the gate of Winchester's ancient St
Cross Hospital at this time, though, for when Defoe visited it
during his tour, he thought its management worth official
enquiry: 'How the revenues of this hospital, which should
maintain the master and thirty private gentlemen . . . is now
reduced to maintain only fourteen, while the master lives in a
figure equal to the best gentlemen in the country, would be well
worth the enquiry of a proper visitor, if such can be named. 'Tis a
thing worthy of complaint, when public charities, designed for
the relief of the poor, are embezzled and deprecated by the rich,
and turned to the support of luxury and pride'.

All this was a recurring theme in the criticism of almshouses as
something similar had been in the criticism of monasteries by
Henry VIII's commissioners, and it was to raise its ugly head
again in the case of St Cross, as we shall see. Doubtless in various
places throughout England, where masters or wardens did not
come before the judgement of twelve jurymen, they were found
guilty enough by twelve old men muttering together in their
coats of alms.

The builder of Frome's so-called Blue House in 1726 turned
down the fashionable courtyard style in favour of a central block
with straight wings either side, these being of three storeys and
very plain, whilst the centre is a little more imposing, with
arched windows and a lantern on the roof, as well as statues of a
charity boy and an old almswoman. For here the almshouse was
combined with a school, and the Bluecoat boys had the advantage of the main block whilst the almshouse inmates – poor old
women of Frome – were relegated to the wings. The school
ceased to be housed here, though, and the whole building was
saved from demolition in recent years only by public protest, and
financial aid eventually secured its renovation and its future.

In Northamptonshire, Deborah Hampden provided a single
cottage in 1725 for 'a poor maiden who shall have lived in good
reputation to the age of forty years'. It was called the Old Maid's
Cottage, and the gift survives in what is now called the Hampden
Cell.

At Houghton in Norfolk, the Prime Minister Robert Walpole

was one of those ruthless landowners of the time who demolished a village because it would ruin the view from the
drawing-room windows of his new mansion, Houghton Hall;
but when he rebuilt the village in formal fashion in 1727 as New
Houghton, it included some single-storey almshouses at the
farthest end from his gates.

Curious architecture at Stidd, Lancashire

At Stidd in Lancashire, John Shireburn, the lord of the manor,
founded the very curious almshouses there in 1728. The stone
building consists of five bays and two storeys, the middle three
bays having an arcade at first floor level, with tall rounded arches
on Tuscan columns and an oddly shaped gable above, forming a
balustraded balcony which is reached by a dominating open
staircase narrowing from the foot. The building apart from this
eccentric centrepiece is as plain as can be. It was intended for five
poor women and the village schoolmistress, and until its modernization in recent years, kind neighbours went each day to
draw buckets of water from the ancient well in the garden, as the
creaking mechanism was too hard for the elderly inmates.

Widows of clergymen were catered for at Mappleton, Derby-shire, in a brick two-storey building with stone dressings and a projecting central bay with giant pilasters; while at Mancetter, Warwickshire, the almshouses founded by James Gramer with a gift of £2,000 in 1728 were actually built in the churchyard – a modest row of single-storey cottages.

The poor of Benington, Lincolnshire, benefited from alms-houses built close to the churchyard in 1728 'by the charity of Mr Wm Porril'. The foundation still survives in this village within sight of Boston's 'Stump', the famous tower of the parish church.

Farther south, in Essex, some of the aged and infirm of Broxbourne and Colchester found new homes in 1728 too. Their benefactor at Broxbourne was Dame Letitia Monson, whose monument with her husband Sir William is in the parish church. The building is plain, of brick on two storeys, with an inscription in a recess above the doorway. At Colchester, Winsley's Almshouses began as a central range with short wings enclosing a courtyard, the wings being so far extended later that, as Pevsner remarks, the courtyard 'seems a cul-de-sac'.

Two ladies of Dunstable, Bedfordshire, founded almshouses for their own sex there in 1728 and 1730. Jane Cart built a row of plain two-storeyed houses in red and blue bricks, next to the school founded by her father William Chew; and her relation Blandina Marshe left money in her will for the erection of a more classical building with a central pediment and a coat of arms. The monuments to Mrs Cart, her husband and her father are in the parish church.

Newbury, Berkshire, had had a strong local tradition of charity since the foundation of St Bartholomew's Hospital there in the twelfth century, possibly by King John. It had long been a wealthy wool town, and although approaching its decline in the eighteenth century, it never overlooked its duty to the poor. In 1729 Thomas Hunt founded a new set of almshouses, and the foundation still exists, though the houses were rebuilt in the early nineteenth century, and now form part of the Newbury Consolidated Charities.

At Brent Eleigh, Suffolk, are the two-storey almshouses of brick founded in 1731 by that same Dr Edward Colman, Fellow of Trinity College, Cambridge, who provided the parish with its

Almshouses beside the churchyard at Mancetter, Warwickshire

former unique library. The books have been dispersed, but the library building remains in the churchyard as testimony, along with the almshouses, to the founder's regard for his native village, and he, too, is buried in the parish church.

Abingdon, Oxfordshire, already graced with fine groups of almshouses close to the church, as we have seen, had the so-called Brick Alley Almshouses added to them in 1718 as an extension of the Christ's Hospital foundation; and then, separated from this close complex where three groups uniquely surround the churchyard, Benjamin Tomkins, of a prominent local family, endowed almshouses for 'four poor men and four poor women for ever'. Built in 1733, the gable-ends of two rows of brick single-storey cottages flanked the street entrance to a narrow courtyard and garden, closed at the opposite end by another gabled wall with an arched doorway which led into a garden.

Down on Romney Marsh, Southland's Hospital was built at New Romney in 1734, and at Blandford Forum in Dorset, a rebuilding of some older dwellings followed in 1736, though they are no longer there. But in that year, something more ambitious occurred at St Albans, as if to give a lift to declining interest and standards in charitable building.

Sarah, Duchess of Marlborough, once 'La Belle Jennings' and Queen Anne's favourite, was now an old dowager of seventy-six, approaching death and making enemies of everyone, being nicknamed 'Her Graceless'. She had made a fortune out of the South Sea Bubble, and perhaps to ease her conscience in her last years she built almshouses at St Albans, where she and the duke had lived for many years before the building of Blenheim Palace. The buildings, in Hatfield Road, were ultimately designed in classical style, round three sides of a lawned courtyard, although originally the duchess had apparently intended not so much an almshouse as a housing estate. She had bought land for the purpose, on which stood a former manor house, and in February 1733 the *London Evening Post* reported that 'several Workmen and other Artificers began to take down divers old buildings at St. Albans by order of her Grace the Dutchess Dowager of Marlborough, in order to raise a noble Building for the relief of 40 poor families of that Town, and her Grace will leave a Sum sufficient to endow it forever'.

The buildings are on a larger scale than anything else we have noticed for some time. The main range has a central three-bay pediment with elaborate arms carved in stone, and the wings, all of two storeys, are plain but dignified. The duchess had a statue of Queen Anne made by the sculptor Rysbrack for the centre of the courtyard, but it was never placed there, the lawn being occupied now by a fine specimen Cedar of Lebanon.

Walpole St Peter in Norfolk and Blewbury in Oxfordshire (Berkshire at that time) acquired modest almshouses in 1737 and 1738, Blewbury's being a single dwelling by the churchyard intended for the oldest man in the village. And at York in the following year, Mary Wandesford founded an almshouse for ten poor Church of England spinsters 'who shall retire from the hurry and noise of the world into a Religious House of Protestant Retirement'. This building, known as the Old Maids' Hospital, is an elegant composition, possibly by John Carr, of red brick with blind arcading and a central pediment bearing a bust of the foundress in a niche.

At Wareham in 1741, John Streche's old foundation of 1418

was rebuilt in Georgian style, also in brick, with a pediment and belfry, though the front is colour-washed now and used as business premises, the 'six antient men and five women' having been moved elsewhere. Then in 1742 came another of the more famous charities, Coram's Foundling Hospital in London. The retired sea captain Thomas Coram built this home for destitute children at Holborn, after being appalled to see dead children lying on dung heaps where they had been thrown to save the cost of burial, some of them unwanted infants murdered by their mothers. Handel, Hogarth and Reynolds were among the hospital's governors. Handel conducted the first performance of *Messiah* in its chapel and Hogarth, who was also a governor of St Bartholomew's, raised funds by persuading his fellow artists to donate works, starting there the first permanent exhibition of English paintings.

Blandina Marshe's foundation at Dunstable

Captain Coram's disinterested concern for the poor is beyond question. His generosity saved many children from a life of crime or prostitution, but led to his own impoverishment, and he spent his last years living on charity himself, dying in 1751 before his hospital was quite complete. The hospital was demolished after 1926, when the foundation was moved to Berkhamsted in

Hertfordshire, and its former site is now a children's playground known as Coram's Fields. But the Thomas Coram Foundation, as it is now called, still exists, caring for the children of poor unmarried mothers, and its modern offices are still near the old site, in Brunswick Square, where paintings and other property of the former hospital include Hogarth's splendidly flamboyant portrait of Captain Coram.

In 1746, a brick and stone house at Petworth, Sussex, originally built early in the seventeenth century, was converted into almshouses and named the Somerset Hospital, after the duke, with a three-storey central block and bay windows – a curious building still in service.

James Millington willed the building of a hospital for sixteen poor people just outside Shrewsbury in 1748, and it had cottages flanking a central school, with a pediment and cupola above a porch with Tuscan columns. The brick building, with its tall chimneys, was much restored at the end of the century, but is of interesting design, the ground-floor latticed windows set in blank round arches and alternating with the smaller windows on the upper floor, above the doors: the whole building being raised on a brick terrace.

From the year 1749, King's Cliffe, Northamptonshire and Beverley, now in Humberside, call for our attention. At King's Cliffe, William Law, who is buried in the churchyard beneath a monument in the shape of a writing desk, founded an almshouse, a charity school and a library in this, the village of his birth. Some would call him eccentric, some saintly, and in truth both would be right, for saintliness is not, and never has been, compatible with what most people regard as normal behaviour. Trained for the Church, but with Jacobite sympathies, Law sacrificed preferment by refusing the oath of allegiance to the House of Hanover on the accession of George I. He wrote theological works, the best known being *A Serious Call to a Devout and Holy Life*, which influenced such widely differing people as the Wesleys, Dr Johnson and Cardinal Newman. Then he settled here with two wealthy ladies from London and began handing out alms to the poor, the news going out on the grapevine so that soon the village was awash with beggars converging on it from every corner of the country. Finally, Rev. Law founded his school for village girls, and his library where

Sarah, Duchess of Marlborough – building almshouses to ease her conscience?

'Books of Piety are here lent to any persons of this or ye neighbouring towns'; and in conjunction with his friend Elizabeth Hutcheson, built the almshouses, a one-storey building of three bays with the school in the middle.

Beverley's almshouses, of the same year as Law's, were founded by Ann Routh, and consisted originally of a single stylish block which has since been extended by the addition of another similar range, all with giant arches.

Salisbury received a new almshouse in 1750, 'built and en-dowed by the liberality of Mr Edward Frowd', which has a very stylish entrance in the centre of its two-storey brick frontage. The doorway has a broken segmental pediment over it, with a flamboyantly adorned inscription, and above that is a Venetian window. The back of the range has a brick arcade and circular windows on the upper floor, and there is a lantern on the roof.

Two years later at Southwark came Hopton's Almshouses (the street near Blackfriars Bridge is also named after their founder). These are brick dwellings on two storeys round a double courtyard, with a committee room at the centre of the main range.

Christopher Tancred, the squire of Whixley in Yorkshire, left the family mansion at his death in 1754 as a hospital for twelve decayed gentlemen, clergymen or commissioned officers, all of whom must belong to the Church of England. He did so out of malice rather than humanitarianism, as he had no children, and no intention of leaving his wealth to his sisters. This was not his only eccentricity. He refused to be buried underground, and for four years his body resided in the hall of the hospital and in the former mansion's wine cellar. Perhaps the 'spirit of place' affected the old men, for they got a reputation for quarrelling and bad behaviour 'highly unedifying to the neighbourhood'. In the nineteenth century, things having got worse rather than better, the Charity Commissioners took the foundation in hand, and in June 1872 the hospital was liquidated and the income converted to out-pensioners.

Northamptonshire came up with an interesting though humble contribution to charitable buildings in 1756 with the Pickering almshouses at Titchmarsh, Northamptonshire, built close to the church and the village green, a single-storey row with thatched roof and dormer windows, and since extended. The local Pickering family was related to the poet Dryden, who was born at Aldwinkle, across the river.

Other famous names are associated with almshouses at Cardington in Bedfordshire, both John Howard, the penal reformer, and his friend Samuel Whitbread, the brewer and Member of Parliament, whose family were lords of the manor, building charitable homes in the village.

In the year of George III's accession, the venerable Mrs Ann

Smyth founded her simple brick almshouses at Ipswich, and at Stoke Poges, Buckinghamshire, five years later Thomas Penn, son of William, the founder of Pennsylvania, replaced the old Hastings almshouses there with a new brick hospital for three poor men and three poor women.

Richmond, Surrey, begot the Queen Elizabeth's Almshouses in 1767, and around 1770 William Mellish, a wealthy merchant of Blyth, Nottinghamshire, built the almshouses there.

Poor folk were apt to benefit from the reluctance of rich men to leave their money to their relations. Thus in 1793 George Jarvis died leaving £100,000 to the poor of three parishes in Herefordshire because he was put out about the marriage of his daughter. The total population of the three parishes was less than nine hundred, and as with William Law's gift at King's Cliffe earlier, the doles did the locality no good, since both poor and greedy from far and wide invaded it on hearing the good tidings, and soon reduced the area to a rural slum.

There was a distinct decline in almshouse building during the remainder of the Georgian period, a fact attributable to several causes, no doubt, chief among which were the social upheaval of

The Duchess of Marlborough's foundation at St Albans

the Industrial Revolution and the economic preoccupation with the Napoleonic Wars. It was a time when riots and machine-breaking led the ruling classes to fear the poor more than pity them, looking at what had happened in revolutionary France.

Northumberland was too far away from all these goings-on to be deterred from normal living, and in 1796, whilst Britain was at odds with France, Holland and Spain, a row of two-storey cottages intended for coal-miners was being built at Heddon-on-the-Wall. But the government took them over for use by refugee French clergymen of Royalist sympathies, and the buildings became known as Frenchmen's Row, never almshouses in the strict sense, but providing roofs over the heads of the needful, all the same.

Caroline, Duchess of Marlborough, built a two-storey block of plain almshouses at Woodstock, Oxfordshire, in 1797, scarcely the equal of her predecessor's contribution at St Albans, and advance warnings of the utilitarian buildings to come were continued at Bedford with two ranges of low brick houses built by Dame Alice Harpur.

There was a good deal of undistinguished rebuilding of older almshouses, too, at this time, such as Archdeacon Pykenham's foundation of the fifteenth century at Hadleigh, Suffolk, and Richard Sloswicke's seventeenth-century hospital at East Retford, Nottinghamshire. But individuality still asserted itself here and there, despite the levelling effects of industrial growth.

Not so fortunate as Frome's Blue School in Somerset were the same town's 'Asylum for poor female children' and the 'Hospital for poor old men'. They were built together in 1803 by Richard Stevens, whose monument in St John's Church has an old man with a stick on one side and two charity boys on the other. (Shouldn't they have been girls? The sculptor, Thomas Cooke, must have been given an inadequate brief, or perhaps he confused Stevens's foundation with the Blue School.) These buildings have been demolished in recent times.

Exmouth in Devon saw in 1811 the foundation of four almshouses for poor elderly spinsters by the Misses Jane and Mary Parminter, cousins who themselves lived in a nearby circular fantasy house called 'A La Ronde'. Their almshouses were built round a tiny chapel, all under one roof, and called 'Point in View', standing on high ground outside the town and looking down across the estuary of the River Exe. The chapel has a little spire with curious triangular windows in it, and was built not so much for the almswomen, as in pursuit of the Parminters' pet preoccupation with the conversion of Jews to Christianity, this being the real 'point-in-view' of their enterprise. One of the spinsters housed there was to be the teacher of six girls – preferably Jewish – for whom the eccentric ladies started a school. This has long ceased to exist, and the school-room is now the chapel vestry. A clause in the will of Jane Parminter, who was buried in the chapel, stated that the oak trees on the estate were to 'remain standing and the hand of man shall not be raised against them, till Israel returns and is restored to the Land of Promise'.

The almshouses have been altered internally to house two ladies in more up-to-date accommodation, but separate bunga-lows have been built in recent years to house other old people, and so the gift of the Misses Parminter continues as a further example of the charity of wealthy women in Georgian England.

At Acton, London, the Goldsmiths' Almshouses of the same year are attractive, with their wings of yellow brick flanking the main range set back from the street, while at Richmond, Surrey,

The Wandesford, or Old Maids', Hospital at York

Michel's Almshouses are plain but dignified, with a central three-bay pediment.

A row of twelve almshouses was founded by Samuel Robinson at Hackney, in 1812, for the 'widows of Dissenting ministers professing Calvinistic doctrines'. When the founder died, twenty-one years later, his tomb was erected on the grass in front of the buildings, causing Mrs Basil Holmes to remark that 'perhaps the widows like to be daily reminded of their benefactor'. Not so, of course. The *benefactor* liked the widows to be daily reminded of him.

York figures again in 1812 with Mrs Dorothy Wilson's Hospital, plain brick with three central blank arches, and the year of Waterloo saw the foundation at Wisbech of Mrs Mayer's attractive two-storey almshouses of brick, called her 'asylum'.

The year 1815 also saw the commencement of a building at Amport in Hampshire, a two-storey block completed in the following year. Was this the place referred to ironically as 'Quality Square' in the village at one time, where the parish housed 'persons whom the churchwardens thought might contaminate the more virtuous inhabitants of the village'?

The following year saw several new foundations in the Thames valley area; at Oxford, Newbury and Sutton Courtenay, for instance. And Deddington, Aynho and Olney also acquired homes for some of their elderly poor. Those built in 1818 at Deddington are especially attractive, with pointed windows and doorways in their walls of the local toffee-coloured ironstone.

Sarratt, Hertfordshire, got the new little brick Baldwin Almshouses opposite the church in 1821. They had originally been founded 400 years ago, but since then the village community had migrated to its new centre round the long green, unfortunately for the old folk, who were left in isolation at what was still the centre of the village when Sir Henry Chauncy published his history of the county in 1700.

Attitudes towards coping with the poor varied, as always. Harriet Martineau was among those who still considered that pauperism should be penalized and the poor made to provide for themselves, and she saw almshouses as evil places, allowing young and able people to evade the responsibility of caring for their parents. Richard Reynolds, the wealthy Quaker iron-

The front of the Foundling Hospital built by Thomas Coram

master, was strongly opposed to what he called 'post-mortuary charity', and he gave his money to the poor while he was still alive, including £4,000 to the Trinity Almshouses and other charities at Bristol, where thousands of poor people lined the streets in respect at his funeral.

In the Midlands, Melton Mowbray, Barrow-on-Soar and Ashby Parva, all in Leicestershire, joined Nottingham and Hereford in building new almshouses, and among other places in the contemporary movement were Bath, Sheffield and Sunderland. The Brownlow lords of the manor at Belton, Lincolnshire, built their model village of stone in the prevailing taste, including the almshouses of 1827. Few almshouses of the time had any architectural distinction, however, and in some cases, though foundations have survived, buildings have gone. Collins' new almshouses at Nottingham, for example, built in 1831, have already become a victim of city redevelopment.

Islington and Lewisham retain their Whittington and Merchant Taylors' almshouses of 1825 and 1826 respectively, both of them following the tradition of ranges enclosing three sides of a courtyard, the former stuccoed and the latter in brick with a central pediment and cupola. Slightly later came the Beeston's Gift Almshouses for the Girdlers' Company at Camberwell (1834) and the Woronzow Almshouses at Marylebone (1836), both stuccoed mock-Tudor buildings. The latter were built near Regent's Park with public subscriptions raised after the Russian ambassador, Count Woronzow, left a bequest of £500 to the parish. On three sides of a courtyard, with a fountain in the centre, they have a chapel in the middle of the main range.

The Salem Almshouses in Barnstaple, Devon, were founded in 1834. Built round an open cobbled courtyard facing Trinity Street, they are in the local brown sandstone on two storeys, and were designed simply, with wooden casement windows.

Saffron Walden and Needham Market brought East Anglia up to date in 1832 and 1836 respectively, without following the urban sham-Gothic tendency. Saffron Walden's brick almshouses have barge-boarded gables characteristic of the area, and gave the little street its name – Almshouse Lane.

Stamford in Lincolnshire gained a crop of little charities in the years between 1770 and 1832, all still in existence under the umbrella title of Stamford Municipal Almshouse Charities. First was Hopkin's Hospital in St Peter's Street; then in 1822 came Snowden's in Scotgate, to be followed ten years later by both Fryer's Callis and Truesdale's Hospital. These were all built in the Gothic style, the last-named round a courtyard.

At Richmond, Surrey, almshouses were founded in 1834 by one rejoicing under the name William Hickey. They were built in the conventional style of the day in grey brick, and still stand, with arms opening out from a main range as if to embrace Richmond Park, only a few yards away.

We can take our leave of this period and look towards the advent of Victorian England at Scarborough, where Wilson's Mariners' Asylum was built in 1836 below the ruins of the old castle. Single-storeyed gabled cottages of brick, these almshouses – like many of those we have noticed from the later Hanoverian period – were dull utilitarian buildings typical of the new industrial approach to housing the poor.

6 Restrained Benevolence in the Victorian Era

In the mid-nineteenth century, allegiance to the Church of England coincided with the extent both of private charity and public poor-relief. Catholic Lancashire's poor law expenditure was under five shillings per head of population in 1834 compared with nearly a pound per head in the counties around London, and the foundation of almshouses also followed this general pattern throughout Queen Victoria's reign.

At the same time, the materialism of the age resulted in a decline in architectural style. Chapels had become confined to foundations of Catholic origin. The founders of charities tended to be the nouveaux riches rather than churchmen or members of the nobility, and their concern was, rightly, to house the old and poor in practical homes, rather than to raise monuments to their own generosity and righteousness, notwithstanding Dickens's assertion in *The Uncommercial Traveller* that 'the question how prosperous and promising the buildings can be made to look in their eyes, usually supersedes the lesser question how they can be turned to the best account for the inmates'. As Trollope suggested, a great battlemented gateway is not necessary for the protection of twelve old men.

The Church's attitude of restrained benevolence is well expressed by Archdeacon Grantly in Trollope's *The Warden*, when one of the bedesmen at Hiram's Hospital has the temerity to suggest that the charity could give him and his fellow inmates a hundred pounds a year: 'When John Hiram built a hospital for worn-out old men, worn-out old labouring men, infirm men past their work, cripples, blind, bedridden, and such like, do you think he meant to make gentlemen of them? Do you think John Hiram intended to give a hundred a year to old single men, who earned perhaps two shillings or half a crown a day for themselves and their families in the best of their time? No, my men, I'll tell you what John Hiram meant; he meant that twelve poor old worn-out labourers, men who could no longer support themselves, who had no friends to support them, who must starve and perish miserably if not protected by the hand of charity; he meant that twelve such men as these should come in here in their poverty and wretchedness, and find within these walls shelter and food before their death, and a little leisure to make their peace with God.'

It should be borne in mind that even the medical hospitals which had proliferated since the Industrial Revolution were charitable institutions whose masters felt themselves responsible for the moral as well as the physical welfare of the poor who came to them as patients. The London Hospital at Whitechapel would not discharge patients until they had been to the hospital chapel to give thanks for their recovery, and the hospital at Exeter prided itself on attending to the 'religion and morals of the laborious poor' as well as to their diseases, whilst they were in its care.

Corruption continued to go hand in hand with the management of funds given to charity, for which no one but the master or warden of an almshouse was usually answerable. When serious disputes arose over founders' intentions, the cost of settling them could be devastating. The Wilkes Almshouses at Leighton Buzzard in Bedfordshire had their entire endowments used up by the cost of proceedings in the Court of Chancery over a period of a quarter of a century, though the foundation survives under the auspices of the local authority.

Winchester's Hospital of St Cross was again in the news shortly after Victoria's accession, and the story provided Trollope with the plot for his novel. Rev. Francis North, a son of the Bishop of Winchester and nephew of the Prime Minister, was made Master of St Cross in 1808, among his other nepotistic sinecures, and he eventually became Earl of Guilford. He did not live on the premises, having a fine enough home in the rectory at Old Alresford, the living of which had also been presented to him by his father the bishop. So he allowed the chaplain of St Cross to live in the master's house – the chaplain being retained because Rev. North's position as master was a lay appointment, not an ecclesiastical one. North exacted a rent from the chaplain for the use of the garden!

The 'New' Almshouses of 1842 at the corner of St John's Churchyard, Devizes, Wiltshire

North's first wife Esther died in 1823, and three years later he married Harriet Warde, thirty-six years younger than himself (he was then fifty-three) and she bore him five children. He acceded to the earldom in the year after his second marriage, and inherited valuable country estates in Kent and Suffolk in addition to the not inconsiderable property and income from his various offices.

Already by this time rumours were in circulation about abuses of the charity's finances. The poet Keats was staying in Winchester in 1819, and wrote of St Cross, which he passed on one of his regular walks, that it was 'a very interesting old place, both for its gothic tower and alms-square and for the appropriation of its rich rents to a relation of the Bishop of Winchester'. It was not until the 1840s, however, that the newspapers got wind of a serious scandal in the offing. The *Hants Independent* alleged in 1843 that the earl had pocketed more than £10,000 which should properly have been for the hospital's charitable work, and the London press then began to show an interest in the story. By 1849, the alleged mishandling of the hospital's funds had become notorious, and having been brought to the notice of Parliament, and the Queen, the Attorney General instituted an enquiry by the Court of Chancery.

The Earl of Guilford, now an old man of seventy-seven, twisted and turned in attempts to release himself from the jurisdiction of the court. He tried to resign, but the new bishop refused him permission until the whole matter had been cleared up. He then protested that his appointment, which for forty years he had maintained was a lay one, was actually an ecclesiastical one, subject only to the bishop's authority. This ruse having failed also, he resigned the rectory of Old Alresford, the house and its contents (which included 700 bottles of port, claret, champagne and other fine wines) being sold by auction; and also resigned his other church livings, apparently in the mistaken impression that these actions would somehow mitigate his offences at St Cross. A letter to *The Times* in 1854 from Rev. R. Lewin of Yateley, one of the St Cross properties, included the following passage:

I have, I think, during the period of my incumbency, upon two occasions, and upon two occasions only, applied for aid in behalf of the parochial poor to the present master of St Cross – in one case, for one guinea per year toward the support of a Sunday School; in the other, in the case of the potato disease – in both cases without success.

His refusal in the second case was contained in a letter, as to style, haughty and absurd; as to matter, ungenerous and unchristian.

The said Rev. the Earl of Guilford has received from this parish, in fines, many thousand pounds.

It was nearly four years before the Court of Chancery delivered its verdict, the Master of the Rolls finding the earl guilty of misappropriating hospital funds. He was ordered to repay certain sums, though these only amounted to around four thousand pounds, accumulated since the case came to court in 1849, whilst estimates of his income from St Cross during his forty-seven years as master varied between £45,000 and £305,700. The earl was finally allowed to resign in 1855, the year Trollope published *The Warden*, and he died six years later.

The former Gascoigne almshouses at Aberford, West Yorkshire

A board of trustees was established to manage the hospital, and the master's salary was reduced.

At about the same time the Charitable Trusts Act was passed, appointing Charity Commissioners to safeguard the proper administration of charities. This was largely at the instigation of Lord Brougham, who had earlier conducted an enquiry aimed at reforming mismanaged charities, especially where money intended for education was not being used to best advantage. It was not long before the Charity Commissioners were at work at Dulwich, where the celibates appointed to Edward Alleyn's foundation were growing wealthy at the expense of the education they were supposed to provide in the school. Dulwich College was created by the establishment's reorganization.

Another case they investigated was Sir John Port's sixteenth-century foundation at Etwall in Derbyshire. It consisted of the almshouses in Etwall and the school at Repton, which was on the verge of becoming an important public school. But the school's board of management included the three oldest inmates of the hospital, who wer: required to attend meetings of the board and make their marks on the school's accounts, and one of them was custodian of the key to the foundation's muniment chest. The Charity Commissioners set about remedying this situation, but met with fierce opposition. There were only fifty-eight labourers in the parish of Etwall, but when attempts were made to get a Bill through Parliament to widen the scope of the almshouses, local people protested that the founder's intention was to benefit residents of Etwall only. They were right, of course. The Charity Commission succeeded in its aims in the end, but had to work with its hands tied, the rope used being the principle of *cy près* enjoined upon it, this being the legal term for following as nearly as possible the founder's original intentions. Opposition to the Charity Commission was nearly always based on a healthy suspicion of bureaucrats and the conviction that a man may do what he likes with his own money.

The age was not wholly preoccupied with ancient foundations, however. Peterborough and Wotton-under-Edge acquired new almshouses in the year of Queen Victoria's accession, 1837, though Wortley's in Peterborough was a replacement of an earlier building. The new foundation in the Cotswold town was by Miss Anne Bearpacker, whose name this modest hospital still rejoices under.

The following year brought new dwellings for the poor and infirm of Cambridge, Durham, Wolviston (Cleveland), Hornchurch (Essex) and East Bilney (Norfolk). Imitation Tudor was the architectural taste of the time, and all of these conformed to it, as did Atwill's Almshouses on the north-west outskirts of Exeter in 1839, though here the red-brick gabled buildings are given some additional interest by being arranged in pairs like semi-detached villas on a terrace above the road level.

At Guildford, Caleb Lovejoy's almshouses were built in

Tudor style in 1839, as were those at Wragby, Lincolnshire in the following year and Chamberlaine's at Bedworth, Warwickshire. Lady Hewley's architect at York also jumped on the mock-Tudor bandwaggon in 1840.

As far apart as Buckden (then in Huntingdonshire) and Sunderland in the Northeast, Devizes in Wiltshire and Ingatestone in Essex, mock-Gothic buildings rose from the ground in the early 1840s, distinguished only by such inspired inscriptions, typical of that dull age, as that at Buckden: 'Industry rewarded, Age protected.' Penge (London) brought a little variation to the scene with its Free Watermen and Lightermen's Almshouses of

Courtyard of the former Vintners' Almshouses (now demolished) in London, probably the model for Dickens's 'Titbull's'

1841, which were built on two storeys round three sides of a courtyard with a battlemented gatehouse; and then followed these up six years later with the King William Naval Asylum, founded by Queen Adelaide, also round a courtyard. Generally, however, new charitable buildings of the period seemed almost predestined to be of the dreary repetitiveness of Tudor themes without the ambitiousness and imagination of the sixteenth century. This was due in part, if not wholly, to the impersonal origin of charitable foundations in the new industrial age. Almshouses now were being built largely by institutions rather than by individual philanthropists. Companies, societies and town and parish councils were the new benefactors, taking over in committee the obligations that used to inspire the wealthy merchant or the rich widow. Gothic windows and doors lent almshouses that hint of ecclesiastical architecture that was considered the proper form for those receiving charity.

Individual landowners and philanthropists still continued to build almshouses here and there, however, particularly as components of their new model or estate villages. Two examples from this period occur in Sussex. At Oving in 1839 picturesque almshouses of flint and stucco were erected as part of the rebuilding of the village by Miss Woods of Shopwyke nearby. And at Tillington, Lord Egremont built almshouses in the following year near the western entrance lodges to Petworth Park.

Sir George Gilbert Scott designed the 1842 Seamen's Houses at Whitby, Yorkshire, in Jacobean style, brick and symmetrical, but not outstanding, and the Tudoresque continued at Spalding and Holbeach, Leeds and Hertford. Not every architect of the period was quite so slavishly imitative. Carpenter's Almshouses at Twickenham were built in 1842 in yellow brick with an arcade at the front and barge-boarded gables; and at Frogmore near St Albans the almshouses were built of red and blue bricks.

In the London docks area, at Woolwich, the modest Parochial Almshouses of 1843 followed the common trend, and at Aberford in Yorkshire George Fowler Jones could not escape it, though his almshouses of the following year were much more ambitious, and built of stone instead of the ubiquitous brick of the Southeast. They were the gift of the Gascoigne family of Lotherton Hall.

Red brick was the material at Ipswich when the Tooley almshouses were rebuilt in Foundation Street in 1846, though the style of the building, with projecting wings, was relieved by flushwork, and the gatehouse (built later) also had exposed timbers. The year 1846 also saw the building of the Tudor-style Crapper almshouses at Whitwick, Leicestershire; the Lloyd almshouses at Abington, Northampton; and the Turner almshouses – the best of these three – in the tiny but charming stone-built village of Trent, near Sherborne in Dorset. These are built round a courtyard with a pump in it.

At Pilton in Devon, a former village now embraced by the northern expansion of Barnstaple, a row of almshouses in Tudor style, built in 1849 of the local red sandstone, gained a little stylishness by facing down the main street with a big archway through the middle, by means of which the parish church is reached. A simple but attractive row of almshouses at West Haddon, Northamptonshire, was the gift in 1846 of William Lovett.

Sir Francis Crossley's palatial almshouses at Halifax

Pugin was one of the few architects who broke the mock-Tudor mould, in designing the so-called St Anne's Bedehouses at Lincoln. Founded by Richard Waldo Sibthorpe, an intermittent Catholic, in 1847, they are an interesting single-storey composition in brick and stone complete with chapel and warden's house. Another Catholic, F. R. Wegg-Prosser, founded the almshouses at Belmont in Herefordshire in 1852.

New buildings at Woburn, Bedfordshire, and Stoneleigh, Warwickshire, in 1850 had failed to bring any fresh imagination to the scene, and Huntingdon and Calcot followed suit in 1852. But at Lambourn in Berkshire, close to the church and vicarage, the rebuilt almshouses of an Elizabethan foundation were given some attractive qualities, with a battlemented façade behind which single-storey almshouses of timber construction are gathered round a cloister. And here and there the tyranny of the Tudor style was at least made worthwhile by a touch of flamboyance, as at Aberford, West Yorkshire, where the Gascoigne almshouses mentioned above had a tower, gables and pinnacles, and at Faversham in Kent, where the almshouses of 1856 are on a larger-than-average scale for the time in brick and stone.

Even London failed to build anything significant, from the architectural point of view, in the early Victorian period, although St Joseph's Almshouses at Hammersmith, built in 1851, made an attractive group of stone in close company with the new Holy Trinity Church; while the old village stocks are companions to the dull red-brick almshouses of 1853 on the village green at Berkswell, West Midlands.

Many of the humble and stereotyped almshouses of the first half of the nineteenth century have been replaced, or are no longer used for charitable purposes. The poor old people for whom they were intended were glad enough to live in them, no doubt. After all, they were quite well off by some standards. Even as late as the Edwardian period, we have the account of a country district nurse who asked a villager if his father was comfortable in the almshouse, and got the reply: 'Well, he'd ought to be, miss. He has a boarded floor.' The housing of the poor in both town and country in early industrial England was, not to put too fine a point on it, squalid, and this generally appalling state of things was sometimes of direct concern to

Sir Joseph Crossley's building at Halifax

charitable foundations. For instance, the manor of Marsh Gibbon in Buckinghamshire had been bestowed by the Pole family in 1441 on their hospital at Ewelme, and 400 years later Sir Henry Acland, who as Regius Professor of Medicine at Oxford was Master of the Trustees, was taken to task for the awful state of the village and the condition of the houses lived in by the village workers who made the charity's profits. But one wonders if the decline in that religiously motivated benevolence of earlier ages, and the lack of architectural imagination, contributed to a general air of discontent among pensioners, showing itself in that tendency toward petty jealousies and complaints so often to be noticed in the old, which Dickens observed so accurately. (Dickens, incidentally, had drawn attention in his journal 'Household Words' to abuses in the management of London's Charterhouse.)

Whereas Trollope had concerned himself in fiction with those in authority over 'Hiram's Hospital', Mr Popular Sentiment, as Trollope called Dickens, concerned himself with something closer to fact in *The Uncommercial Traveller*, regarding the inmates of what he called 'Titbull's Alms-Houses', based on an institution in London. He first encountered an old man grumbling about the inadequacies of the pump from which the almspeople had to draw their water, and later described two 'little stooping blear-eyed old men of cheerful countenance, and they hobble up and down the court-yard wagging their chins and talking together quite gaily. This has given offence, and has, moreover, raised the question whether they are justified in passing any other windows than their own'.

Dickens also gives a nice glimpse of the rooms in which the nine old ladies of this almshouse lived. 'Generally an antiquated chest of drawers is among their cherished possessions; a tea-tray always is. I know of at least two rooms in which a little tea-kettle of genuine burnished copper vies with the cat in winking at the fire; and one old lady has a tea-urn set forth in state on the top of her chest of drawers, which urn is used as her library, and contains four duodecimo volumes, and a black-bordered newspaper giving an account of the funeral of Her Royal Highness the Princess Charlotte.'

Dickens goes on to tell the delightful story of a late romance blossoming between one of the resident ladies and a Greenwich pensioner: 'Resignation of a dwelling is of very rare occurrence in Titbull's. A story does obtain there, how an old lady's son once drew a prize of Thirty Thousand Pounds in the Lottery, and presently drove to the gate in his own carriage, with French Horns playing up behind, and whisked his mother away, and left ten guineas for a Feast. But I have been unable to substantiate it by any evidence, and regard it as an Alms-House Fairy Tale. It is curious that the only proved case of resignation happened within my knowledge.

'It happened on this wise. There is a sharp competition among the ladies respecting the gentility of their visitors, and I have so often observed visitors to be dressed as for a holiday occasion, that I suppose the ladies to have besought them to make all possible display when they come. In these circumstances much excitement was one day occasioned by Mrs. Mitts receiving a visit from a Greenwich Pensioner. He was a Pensioner of a bluff and warlike appearance, with an empty coat-sleeve, and he was got up with unusual care; his coat-buttons were extremely bright, he wore his empty coat-sleeve in a graceful festoon, and he had a walking-stick in his hand that must have cost money. When, with the head of his walking-stick, he knocked at Mrs.

Mitt's door – there are no knockers in Titbull's – Mrs. Mitts was overheard by a next-door neighbour to utter a cry of surprise expressing much agitation; and the same neighbour did afterwards solemnly affirm that when he was admitted into Mrs. Mitts's room, she heard a smack. Heard a smack which was not a blow.

'There was an air about this Greenwich Pensioner when he took his departure, which imbued all Titbull's with the conviction that he was coming again. He was eagerly looked for, and Mrs. Mitts was closely watched. In the meantime, if anything could have placed the unfortunate six old gentlemen at a greater disadvantage than that at which they chronically stood, it would have been the apparition of this Greenwich Pensioner. They were well shrunken already, but they shrunk to nothing in comparison with the Pensioner. Even the poor old gentlemen themselves seemed conscious of their inferiority, and to know submissively that they could never hope to hold their own against the Pensioner with his warlike and maritime experience in the past, and his tobacco money in the present: his chequered career of blue water, black gunpowder, and red bloodshed for England, home, and beauty.

'Before three weeks were out, the Pensioner reappeared. Again he knocked at Mrs. Mitts's door with the handle of his stick, and again was he admitted. But not again did he depart alone; for Mrs. Mitts, in a bonnet identified as having been re-embellished, went out walking with him, and stayed out till the ten o'clock beer, Greenwich time.

'There was now a truce, even as to the troubled waters of Mrs. Saggers's pail; nothing was spoken of among the ladies but the conduct of Mrs. Mitts and its blighting influence on the reputation of Titbull's. It was agreed that Mr. Battens "ought to take it up", and Mr. Battens was communicated with on the subject. That unsatisfactory individual replied "that he didn't see his way yet", and it was unanimously voted by the ladies that aggravation was in his nature.

'How it came to pass, with some appearance of inconsistency, that Mrs. Mitts was cut by all the ladies and the Pensioner admired by all the ladies, matters not. Before another week was out, Titbull's was startled by another phenomenon. At ten o'clock in the forenoon appeared a cab, containing not only the

Gabled almshouses of Cotswold stone at Eastleach

Greenwich Pensioner with one arm, but, to boot, a Chelsea Pensioner with one leg. Both dismounting to assist Mrs. Mitts into the cab, the Greenwich Pensioner bore her company inside, and the Chelsea Pensioner mounted the box by the driver: his wooden leg sticking out after the manner of a bowsprit, as if in jocular homage to his friend's sea-going career. Thus the equipage drove away. No Mrs. Mitts returned that night.

'What Mr. Battens might have done in the matter of taking it up, goaded by the infuriated state of public feeling next morning, was anticipated by another phenomenon. A Truck, propelled by the Greenwich Pensioner and the Chelsea Pensioner, each placidly smoking a pipe, and pushing his warrior breast against the handle.

'The display on the part of the Greenwich Pensioner of his "marriage-lines", and his announcement that himself and friend had looked in for the furniture of Mrs. G. Pensioner, late Mitts, by no means reconciled the ladies to the conduct of their sister; on the contrary, it is said that they appeared more than ever exasperated. Nevertheless, my stray visits to Titbull's since the date of this occurrence, have confirmed me in an impression that it was a wholesome fillip. The nine ladies are smarter, both in mind and dress, than they used to be, though it must be admitted that they despise the six gentlemen to the last extent. They have a much greater interest in the external thoroughfare too, than they had when I first knew Titbull's. And whenever I chance to be leaning my back against the pump or the iron railings, and to be talking to one of the junior ladies, and to see that a flush has passed over her face, I immediately know without looking round that a Greenwich Pensioner has gone past.'

The consensus of opinion is that Dickens based his 'Titbull's' on the former Vintners' Almshouses in Mile End Road. He says that they 'are in the east of London, in a great highway, in a poor busy and thronged neighbourhood', and that the pump stood 'just inside the gate' after descending three stone steps from the street, which was fronted by iron railings. In all this they were distinctly similar to the Trinity Almshouses at the junction with Whitechapel Road, but as Dickens does not refer to any statues in the courtyard, the preference for Vintners' as the model is probably correct, especially as Dickens says the courtyard was paved, and referred to an inscription stone with sculptured drapery above it. The courtyard of the Vintners' was narrower than the Trinity, but it had a chapel similarly placed, closing the courtyard at the opposite end from the street entrance, with single-storey houses of brick along either side, and climbing plants growing up the walls. Dickens suggests that it was founded early in the eighteenth century for nine poor women and six poor men.

The Charity Commissioners persisted in their doctrine, in answer to the supposed sanctity of a benefactor's wishes, that ancient endowments should be made to serve the living rather than the dead, but they experienced great difficulties in putting their theories into practice, and sometimes they could make no headway at all. They failed to reform Christ's Hospital at Sherburn, near Durham, for instance, which had an income of £4,700 from land and mining interests. The Master, George Faber, a clergyman appointed by the Bishop of Durham, pocketed what was left of this after running expenses. He got around £3,000 a year without the obligation, as the Commissioners observed, 'to perform any duty of importance'. The Commissioners wanted to abolish the requirement for a clerical master and divert his income to a medical hospital as the nearest equivalent to the medieval founder's concern for sufferers from leprosy. They found themselves powerless to push this reform through, however, and further evidence of their emasculation came with their efforts at Browne's Hospital at Stamford, when they attempted to interfere with the board's determination to appoint a new confrater at a stipend of £200, even though the agricultural depression had rendered the foundation incapable of supporting the twelve almsmen.

Thomas Love Peacock poked fun at the Charity Commissioners in *Crotchet Castle*. The Reverend Dr Folliott, in company with the churchwardens, receives a visit from the commissioners, who have come to enquire into 'the state of the public charities of this village':

The Rev Dr Folliott: The state of the public charities, sir, is exceedingly simple. There are none. The charities here are all private, and so private, that I for one know nothing of them.

First Commissioner: We have been informed, sir, that there is an annual rent charged on the land of Hautbois, for the endowment and repair of an almshouse.

The Rev Dr Folliott: Hautbois! Hautbois!

First Commissioner: The manorial farm of Hautbois, now occupied by Farmer Seedling, is charged with the endowment and maintenance of an almshouse.

The Rev Dr Folliott (to the Churchwarden): How is this, Mr Bluenose?

First Churchwarden: I really do not know, sir. What say you, Mr Appletwig?

Mr Appletwig (parish-clerk and schoolmaster; an old man): I do remember, gentlemen, to have been informed, that there did stand, at the end of the village, a ruined cottage, which had once been an almshouse, which was endowed and maintained, by an annual revenue of a mark and a half, or one pound sterling, charged some centuries ago on the farm of Hautbois; but the means, by the progress of time, having become inadequate to the end, the almshouse tumbled to pieces.

First Commissioner: But this is a right which cannot be abrogated by desuetude, and the sum of one pound per annum is still chargeable for charitable purposes on the manorial farm of Hautbois.

The Rev Dr Folliott: Very well, sir.

Mr Appletwig: But, sir, the one pound per annum is still received by the parish, but was long ago, by an unanimous vote in open vestry, given to the minister.

The Three Commissioners (unâ voce): The minister!

First Commissioner: This is an unjustifiable proceeding.

Second Commissioner: A misappropriation of a public fund.

Third Commissioner: A flagrant perversion of a charitable donation.

The Rev Dr Folliott: God bless my soul, gentlemen! I know nothing of this matter. How is this, Mr Bluenose? Do I receive this one pound per annum?

First Churchwarden: Really, sir, I know no more about it than you do.

Mr Appletwig: You certainly receive it, sir. It was voted to one of your predecessors. Farmer Seedling lumps it in with his tithes.

First Commissioner: Lumps it in, sir! Lump in a charitable donation!

Second and Third Commissioners: Oh-oh-oh-h-h!

First Commissioner: Reverend sir, and gentlemen, officers of this parish, we are under the necessity of admonishing you that this is a most improper proceeding; and you are hereby duly admonished accordingly. Make a record, Mr Milky.

Mr Milky (writing): The clergyman and churchwardens of the village of Hm-m-m-m- gravely admonished. Hm-m-m-m.

By the middle of the century, a new social conscience was beginning to surface, especially among wealthy industrialists, and the new model villages of the time usually included alms-houses, such as those at Saltaire, Sir Titus Salt's village outside Bradford. These – forty-five in all – were designed like villas in the same Italianate style as Salt's wool mill and his employees' houses, and the qualifications for admission were 'good moral character, and incapacity for labour by reason of age, disease or infirmity'.

Outside the old city walls of Chester, almshouses connected with the medieval St John's Hospital of 1232 were rebuilt in 1854. The surviving chapel, known as Little St John, had been shared with the nearby Bluecoat School and the city gaol. But at Halifax, the lavish showed signs of returning, in Nathaniel

Waterhouse's gabled ranges of Tudor Gothic built near the town centre in 1855, and the almshouses of the Crossley family of carpet manufacturers on the outskirts. Sir Francis Crossley's of 1855 and Joseph Crossley's of 1863 were still imitation Tudor in style, but the latter was arranged round a large open courtyard. An element of rivalry seemed to be returning to charitable endowments, and perhaps a fresh input of pride and respectability was brought to the provision of homes for the poor and infirm by hints of the traditional royal links. The almshouses built in Victoria Street at Windsor in 1862 were ordinary enough, to be sure, but at Cambridge, a large new building in multi-coloured brick, notwithstanding its singular unattractiveness, was given the name Royal Albert Almshouses.

The original Dame Mico's Almshouses of the Mercers' Company in White Horse Street, Stepney, were rebuilt in 1857, and are now used as a school, with eighteenth-century statues of two charity children. But the approach to the almshouses was

Almshouses designed by Sir George Gilbert Scott at Sandbach, Cheshire

through a graveyard which, as Mrs Holmes, author of *The London Burial Grounds*, remarked, 'cannot be a lively outlook for the pensioners'.

In fact, though, before the growth of public cemeteries in Victorian England, many almshouses had their own burial grounds, especially in London, where the churchyards were notoriously overcrowded and disgraceful. Among others, the College of God's Gift at Dulwich, the Goldsmiths' Almshouses at Shoreditch, St Saviour's at Southwark, and Morden College, Blackheath, had their own private graveyards, the last-named being a quarter of an acre in extent.

The possession of a private burial ground in the Middle Ages, and probably later, could bring financial benefits to the hospital, since its 'use' was not necessarily confined to inmates. It may be that private cemeteries began with the lazar houses, but there is a record of a Bristol man requesting burial in the cemetery of St Mark's Hospital, to which he left a welcome legacy in return for the favour, and no doubt there were other such instances.

At Rochester in 1858, the old Watts charity hospital of the sixteenth century, known as the Travellers' Rest, was rebuilt some distance away, in Maidstone Road, as the Watts Almshouses. This building was done in Jacobean style, a long symmetrical range to accommodate eighteen pensioners.

South Weald, Essex, and Broughton, Oxfordshire, brought a little architectural imagination to new almshouses in 1858 and 1859 respectively. Mr S. S. Teulon designed much new building at South Weald, including the rebuilt church, and his almshouses of brick are stepped down a sloping site in an attractive group with a chapel in the middle. At Broughton, the almshouses founded by Elizabeth Bradford Wyatt are two houses of two storeys with a gabled wall between.

Bristol's apparently insatiable appetite for creating charitable institutions continued with Foster's Almshouses, built from 1861 over a period of several years in French Gothic, a distinct departure from the prevailing fashion.

The local lords of the manors founded almshouses in 1862 at Revesby, Lincolnshire (due for restoration at the time of writing), and at Little Tew, Oxfordshire, the latter approached via a lychgate and forming a pleasant group with the school near the manor house.

Whatever the reason, there was a distinct raising of tone in almshouses from the 1860s, nowhere typified more clearly than at Winchcombe in Gloucestershire, where Sir George Gilbert Scott designed the picturesque Sudeley Almshouses of 1865, founded by John Dent, and stone-built with gabled porches on a sloping terrace at right angles to the main street. And at Watford, almshouses built in 1863 for the Salters' Company were pleasantly above average, though still almost slavishly following the Tudor style in red brick. Earl Spencer of Althorp built the Tudor-style gabled almshouses at Church Brampton, Northamptonshire in 1860.

To the north-west of Bournemouth, which had a population of only about two thousand at the time, the very rich Georgina Charlotte Talbot and her sister Mary Anne founded their Talbot model village in the 1830s, which included almshouses by 1862 as well as farms and cottages, church and school. Designed by Christopher Crabbe Creeke, the Surveyor of Bournemouth, the almshouses for seven married couples or single persons were built in stone with curious round-arched two-light windows with diamonds in the spandrels, in gables flanked by smaller gables above the doors.

At Barnet, the Leathersellers' Almshouses were built in 1866 to replace the original buildings in Bishopsgate, which were one of the very few to be built during the course of the Dissolution in 1544. At Eastleach, Gloucestershire, a single-storey row of gabled stone almshouses with wooden porches proclaims itself the gift of William Atkinson in memory of Robert Gardner.

Not many of the latest foundations could escape from the stereotyped form of half a century. Berkshire was let down by Newbury, Reading and Wantage in quick succession; Yorkshire by Scarborough; Cheshire by Sandbach; East Anglia by King's Lynn and Woodbridge; Wiltshire by Zeals, although Trowbridge came up with an interesting building in 1867 in its Union Street Almshouses, with a stone arcade on the ground floor and a timber balcony above.

No one let the side down at Fulham. Sir William Powell founded his almshouses close to the churchyard there – still outside the main London build-up then – in 1869. The single-storey cottages are built on an L-shaped plan round an attractive courtyard garden, and have steep roofs with dormer windows –

Sir William Powell's foundation at Fulham

a homely group owing little to Tudor forms. Near the church-yard end is a heavily ornamented Victorian turret, with figures of Faith, Hope and Charity, among others, and the inscription 'God's Providence, Our Inheritance'. The providence, of course, was not God's, but Sir William's.

Leyland gave Lancashire a little flush of charity with its so-called 'Fairy Tale Cottages' in red brick, and the Osbaldestone Almshouses of 1870, with their barge-boarded porches and dormer windows; while at Macclesfield in 1871 the Stanley Almshouses continued the Gothic theme and at Capel in Surrey the stone-built Webb Almshouses of the same year were what Pevsner calls the most striking building in the village street. At Godstone, Sir George Gilbert Scott designed the St Mary's Homes in asymmetrical style and attractive half-timbered con-struction. At Finedon, Northamptonshire, the model village being developed by William Mackworth-Dolben in mock-Tudor style included a row of almshouses with dormer win-dows. At South Dalton, then in Yorkshire's East Riding, a nice group was built in 1873 with timber verandahs and dormers, and with a stone chapel adjoining. Moreton's Almshouses of 1874 at Westerham in Kent were given a stone ground floor with half-timbering above. Salisbury kept up its outstanding record

Moreton's Almshouses at Westerham, Kent

of housing the aged poor of the city with the rebuilding in 1875 of Hussey's almshouses, which are now incorporated with several other foundations under the City Almshouse and Welfare Charities.

Many places, of course, continued to pursue the heavy and ugly Victorian Gothic in the 1870s – Worcester, Aylesbury and Burton-on-Trent among them. Felsted's almshouses of 1878 in Essex are arranged round an open courtyard. The Poynder Almshouses of the same year at Hilmarton, Wiltshire, were unexceptional, but at Guildford, the new buildings completed in the following year for the Onslow foundation, to be moved out of London, were more original – asymmetrical single-storey dwellings stepped down near one end with a curious double gable, and attractive windows.

The Charity Commission, meanwhile, was doing its best to bring some order to the chaos of private charity, which had inevitably resulted in some old folk living in relative luxury while others barely had the means of subsistence. The various almshouses in Norwich, for instance, had an income of £10,000 between them; those of Coventry only £1,000. One old hospital at York had so much income in relation to its number of inmates that each of them received £94 a year around 1849, which was deemed by Lord Brougham's committee 'an income unnecessarily and mischievously large for persons in that station of life'. York was especially noted for its almshouses, of which there were twenty separate groups at the end of the century. The Charity Commission made several changes in their administration, but failed because of local opposition in their aim of amalgamating them all into a united charity in order to provide more equal benefit for all the city's poor old people.

There was a growing conviction that the collective responsibility of improving living conditions for the whole population must replace private and local provision for the fortunate few. 'Surely,' said Joseph Chamberlain in 1885, 'there is some reason to doubt the perfection of our system when in this, the richest country in the world, one in thirty of the population at every moment are unable to obtain the means of subsistence without recourse to the parish.'

The Charity Organisation Society had been set up in 1869 to co-operate with the Poor Law and charitable foundations in

*Almshouses for retired royal servants at Whippingham,
Isle of Wight*

improving the condition of the poor and to correct 'the malad-
ministration of charity', but it was a moralizing body of largely
religious volunteers, which opposed state action in relieving
poverty.

'It is legislation that is wanted, not almsgiving', wrote George
Sims in *How the Poor Live*, and the cry was echoed by Charles
Booth, the Webbs, Bernard Shaw and many others who saw the
old Tudor call to alms as a totally inadequate and outdated
response to poverty, practised and approved by people who, as
Shaw was to put it in *The Intelligent Woman's Guide to
Socialism and Capitalism*, 'believed firmly that the world can be
made good by independent displays of coercive personal
righteousness'.

In 1880, nevertheless, Queen Victoria followed the example
of her royal predecessors with a foundation at Whippingham on
the Isle of Wight. She built almshouses here for retired royal
servants of Osborne House. The almshouses were erected opposite the rebuilt church which Prince Albert had designed, and
are one of the most striking sets of modern almshouses anywhere
in England. They are built of bright red brick and matching red
tiles on a pale stone terrace, with much patterning in both the
brickwork and on the roofs, and with tall chimneys, many
unequal gables, and terracotta coats of arms. The windows, with
wooden mullions and transoms, are glazed in small lozenge
patterns and stand out in white, and although the front, overlooking a lawn and shrubbery, is symmetrical, the variety of

shapes and angles lend these buildings an almost medieval look of homely disorder.

Even the City of Westminster could scarcely match these, though its United Almshouses of 1881, not far from Buckingham Palace, were built in red brick round an open court with Dutch gables, and a lantern on the roof of the main range. The royal example was followed in spirit, if not in style, at Kendal in Cumbria, the date of the foundation being proclaimed in its title, the Sleddall Victoria Jubilee Almshouses.

At Hull, the 1884 Trust Almshouses on the north-western outskirts achieved some attractiveness with timber-framed gables above brick walls, round a turfed court entered via a towered gatehouse. Wotton-under-Edge in Gloucestershire deserves remark once again, the small Cotswold wool town where we have already noticed the Perry and the Bearpacker foundations having also benefited from a gift of Rowland Hill, the Calvinist preacher, whose almshouses were rebuilt, with their little timber verandahs, in 1887, close to the Tabernacle which bears his name.

Lord Aldenham built almshouses at Elstree (London), and at Ickburgh in Norfolk. Claire, Lady Ashburton, of the Baring banking family, built almshouses with half-timbered gables, keeping up the long tradition of private charities, whilst at Waddesdon in Buckinghamshire, Baron Ferdinand Rothschild rebuilt the old Goodwyn Almshouses in plain style in 1893, as part of his new model village. At Radwinter, Essex, Eden Nesfield built new almshouses in his redevelopment of the village in 1887, replacing Miss Bullock's original foundation there.

When the People's Palace was built in London's Mile End Road in 1885, as an entertainment centre for the East End, it involved the demolition of the Bancroft Almshouses, and there was a threat to demolish the late seventeenth-century Trinity Almshouses, farther along the road, as well, but fortunately these were saved. The old Bancroft foundation was one of those which had its own graveyard, but St Benet's Church and vicarage were built on the site even before the People's Palace took the place of the old folks' homes.

The Skinners' Company almshouses at Palmer's Green, built in 1895, made an interesting if not exactly beautiful mixture of details, with a copper cupola on their steep tiled roofs and timber arcades below. Soon afterwards, James Marshall of Marshall & Snelgrove gave land and money at Mill Hill, then in Middlesex, for the development of a garden estate for the Linen and Woollen Drapers' Homes, with brick and timber cottages of both one and two storeys.

But it was Birmingham, of all places, that saw the nineteenth century and the Victorian age out with a little touch of class, in the almshouses built in George Cadbury's model village of Bournville, following the precedent set at Bradford by Sir Titus Salt. The Bournville almshouses are single-storey dwellings ranged round a large lawned courtyard, and built in brick and stone with half-timbered gables and mullioned windows. But were not utopian villages such as Saltaire and Bournville, with better housing for all classes of workers as their priorities, precursors of that Welfare State which makes all almshouses anachronisms?

7 Almshouses Today – A Survival Story

Certainly the Edwardian period produced scarcely a single almshouse of note, except at Hull, a city already a haven of civilization according to Dr Johnson's standards. In 1909 Hull begat the Pickering Almshouses, homely single-storey terraced cottages of brick and stone with gables and loggias. By that time, Poor Law Relief and the abominable workhouse test had been replaced by Old Age Pensions – 'an honourable sustenance for deserving old age', in Lloyd George's words – and no doubt there was some hesitation on the part of the wealthy as to whether the tradition of private charity had not now been rendered totally obsolete.

Public agitation sometimes excited by allegations of improper administration of private charities faded away with increasing State responsibility, and the Charity Commission became a sort of routine office of good works, restrained by the *cy près* principle from diverting capital away from the purposes the original philanthropists had thought fit to support. At one time, when the Commission had found some charities with surplus funds, it had often diverted this income to education, even when the original benefactor had left his money entirely for the elderly poor and with no mention of education in his bequest. But when the State assumed responsibility for schools, it did not return to the almshouses the capital which rightly belonged to them, and thus hived off by devious means a good deal of the money meant for housing the old and infirm, and left many almshouses impoverished.

We have noticed throughout the history of English almshouses the rival claims of the very old and the very young on the funds available for helping the poor. Many philanthropists over the centuries provided almshouses and schools in single foundations, as we have seen, but very often it was a case of financing either one or the other, and children sometimes took precedence over pensioners. By making education a State responsibility, such rivalry has been ended, but it is a legitimate question whether it is right that the care of so many who have served the country all their working lives in the past should still be dependent on private charity, any more than the education of those who are expected to serve the country all their working lives in the future.

It may be difficult for the purist to reconcile the image of a cloistered community of old people, who are heirs to the estate of their medieval benefactor but have no say whatever in its disposal, with the modern provision of Old Age Pensions, National Health, Supplementary Benefits, Help the Aged, Meals on Wheels, and all the other appurtenances of public and state-controlled modern welfare. But a romantic regard for outdated institutions persists throughout society, and helps to keep the practice of private charity alive, even if it ought in theory to be no longer strictly necessary. The philanthropic impulse has been strong during most periods of English history.

Nowhere is the strength of this tradition seen more clearly than at Rochester, where the very striking new Foord Almshouses were built in 1926, with both one- and two-storeyed ranges round a huge open-ended courtyard, and with wall-paintings and stained glass in the hall. This throw-back to earlier forms was designed by Guy Dawber and enlarged in 1931 to accommodate sixty-three people. As Pevsner puts it: 'Indoor sanitation, but two pumps. That sums it up. What fun it must have been to fetch water by pail! What fun to peer out of a mullioned window!'

The present century has, however, been marked more by demolition of redundant buildings, and much rebuilding and improvement in standards of accommodation, than by the appearance of new foundations. We have noticed many examples of rebuilding, extensions, and transfers to new quarters, and to the disappearance of almshouses at places such as Glastonbury, Exeter and elsewhere already commented on, may be added the demolition of almshouses at Poole in Dorset, West Lavington in Wiltshire and other places. Poole, for instance, in 1971 demolished its Rogers' Almshouses which had been built in the earliest years of James I's reign and kept up as late as 1927, then abandoned, along with other worthwhile buildings in the town.

Sometimes old almshouses can produce interesting finds in the course of repair or demolition. At Heavitree, Devon (now part of Exeter) workmen making building alterations to the fifteenth-century Livery Dole Almshouses in 1849 found a charred stake which is believed to be the one at which a schoolmaster named Benet was burnt for his religious beliefs in 1533. The ring and bolt for the chain were still attached to it.

At Castlemorton, Hereford and Worcester, an old house of cruck construction which had been converted into an almshouse with many brick chimneys has been reclaimed as a private dwelling, and the same fate befell eighteenth-century alms-houses at Redbourne, Humberside.

Nantwich and London (Poplar) are among places guilty of allowing fine old almshouses to fall into dereliction, whilst Edgware's almshouses founded by Samuel Atkinson in 1680 were among the victims of wartime bomb damage.

At Watford, the nineteenth-century Morrison Almshouses were demolished in 1965, though the foundation survives, and in the same town the former Longley Almshouses have recently been sold.

None of these buildings were such spectacular losses as the Royal Naval Hospital or those victims of the Dissolution like the Savoy or York's St Leonard's, but in a more conservation-conscious age some of them ought to have been better cared for. Almshouses are, after all, among the finest surviving examples of vernacular architecture from all ages and were, by their very nature, built to last. On the plus side, however, parts of many older almshouses are now opened to the public at certain times as buildings of historic interest.

Not that almshouse building is entirely a thing of the past. Plenty of other new buildings besides Hull's and Rochester's have gone up in the present century. Worcester acquired new buildings for the Laslett foundation there in 1912, in a timber-framed and brick construction designed by one of those many firms of local architects throughout the country which were now becoming involved in replacing old almshouses along with other urban redevelopment.

The removal of the Ironmongers' Company almshouses from Shoreditch to Mottingham has already been mentioned. The new buildings in Kent were built in 1912 to a design by George Hubbard, and the original statue of their founder, Sir Robert Geffrye, stands in the grounds.

One of the most notable twentieth-century developments has been the Durham Aged Mineworkers' Homes Association, which provides a huge number of homes for retired miners in that part of England. The Association was actually founded in the latter years of the nineteenth century, and the first houses were occupied in 1899, but the movement is essentially modern in spirit and properly belongs to this chapter. The vision behind this association was that of Joseph Hopper, a miner and quarryman himself, who battled for years against prejudice and ridicule to get his idea off the ground. 'The four shillings per week', he said in a speech in 1896, 'which our aged miners receive from the Superannuation Fund is helpful (but) it is utterly insufficient to provide an aged couple with food, firing, shelter and clothing in a reasonable manner; and in order to assist our superannuated miners we resolve to push forward a movement for the establishment of Aged Miners' Homes.'

In due course, the homes began to appear in the mining villages of Durham – sometimes existing colliery dwellings which had been purchased and renovated; sometimes purpose-built cottages. Joseph Hopper died in 1909, but not before he had seen his plans materialize, and his associates continued the work, which resulted – as his lifelong friend John Oxberry put it 'in dotting the North of England with havens of rest for superannuated mineworkers, such as no other body of workmen has ever possessed'.

The Association's register of tenants in 1915 included many who had spent working lives of such length in the mining industry as appall us now, such as Thomas Spring, W. Richardson and S. Beresford, who had all worked for seventy years, at Tanfield, Ryhope and Craghead respectively. By 1924 the Durham Aged Miners' Homes Association had more than a thousand occupied dwellings, and is still a powerful force, throughout Durham and Tyne and Wear, in housing retired couples from the local mining industry.

At Painswick, Gloucestershire, Sidney Barnsley, one of that

group of local craftsmen-disciples of William Morris, designed the Gyde Almshouses, founded by a surgeon whose tomb is in the churchyard, and built in 1916 – ten semi-detached cottages of Cotswold limestone. But in 1913 at Cranage, Cheshire, the old mock-Tudor style had been resorted to yet again in the brick almshouses there.

Meanwhile, in Surrey, a new form of almshouse concept was taking shape near Cobham. Whiteley Village was the legacy of Sir William Whiteley, the retailer who was murdered by a man who claimed to be his heir. A whole new village, largely inspired by the example of James Marshall at Mill Hill, was built on 225 acres of land surrounded by a road forming an octagon. Completed in 1921, the village housing was designed by several architects taking a section each, divided by roads radiating out from the centre. They were restricted only by the material they were to use, which was brick. As many as 350 pensioners of the agricultural and commercial professions were housed in a community which, in some measure, reconciled the traditional view of almshouses to the modern Welfare State. The residents, who pay a small rent, live in pleasant surroundings which neither isolate nor institutionalize them. A village shop, social club and library are among the facilities, and a statue of Whiteley stands at the centre of the octagon.

In 1927 at Cirencester, Norman Jewson – another of the Morris-inspired Cotswold group – designed the new stone almshouses for Christopher Bowly's foundation, and followed them seven years afterwards with another group in the name of Mrs Bowly.

At Thorpeness, on the coast of Suffolk near Aldeburgh, the wealthy writer Glencairn Stuart Ogilvie, a relative of Sir J. M. Barrie, began the building of a small new seaside resort in garden village form in 1910. The promotional literature described it as 'the home of Peter Pan', and it had a lake with islands named after Barrie's characters, as well as some picturesque, if bizarre, buildings. In 1928 an attractive set of almshouses was built there, to the design of W. G. Wilson, with a road going through the centre, and the foundation is now known as the Margaret Ogilvie Almshouse Charity.

At Bibury in Gloucestershire, incidentally, the village which William Morris considered the most beautiful in England,

Homes built for retired miners at Boldon, Tyne & Wear

stands the Jesus Almshouse, a single cottage built by Hugh
Westwood, and unobserved by the throngs of visitors who gaze
at Arlington Row and watch the trout in the stream.

At South Molton in Devon, where the poor old folk had had to
live with their best potential benefactor Hugh Squier's preference for the young, George Thomas Cock and his wife Bridget
made bequests in 1930 by which the town's Cottage Homes
were built – a long crescent of single-storey cottages with roofs
of graded stone tiles and inset wooden porches, with a through
archway to the back in the middle of the row. They are situated
very conveniently for the cemetery but not for the shops.

Before the Second World War, the new Shireburn almshouses
were built at Hurst Green near Stoneyhurst, Lancashire, replacing earlier buildings of the Catholic family's foundation at
Longridge. And the Portal family was responsible for the 1939
almshouses at Laverstoke, Hampshire – fanciful half-timbered
and gabled dwellings with thatched roofs.

In 1947, the Survey Committee of the Nuffield Foundation,
under the chairmanship of B. S. Rowntree of the Quaker family
of York, published a report *Old People*, in which it found that

there were nearly 1,500 residence charities accommodating over 22,000 people. These included religious organizations like the Salvation Army as well as communal old people's homes. But the endowed almshouses accounted for the largest proportion of residents – around 12,000 at that time. The Nuffield Foundation established the National Corporation for the Care of Old People as a direct result of this survey, and also achieved, to a slightly lesser degree, what the Charity Commission had signally failed to manage – some amalgamation of municipal charities in York, intended to serve as an example of forward thinking for the whole country.

Aneurin Bevan's National Assistance Act of 1948 also took note of this state of affairs and invited almshouses to regard themselves as willing partners of the State in carrying out its new welfare policies. The National Assistance Board, with its supplementary allowances to people in need, relieved almshouses of the financial burdens they faced with shrinking incomes and rising housing standards. They were thus able to charge small rents in many cases, or expect residents to make some contribution to their own maintenance, such as paying for their electricity, or for a home help if needed, or meals on wheels. The pensions have also meant that some residents have been able to put a little money by these days. (I was told in one almshouse of an old lady who had died leaving £700 in cash under her bed, and although this is not one of Dickens's 'Almshouse Fairy Tales', it is hardly a common occurrence.) In turn, this has meant that the governing bodies of almshouses have been able to devote more of their funds to the upkeep of buildings and improvement of housing standards. The majority of almshouses now have, or are in process of installing, central heating.

The Association of London Almshouses was formed after the Second World War, with financial aid from the Nuffield Foundation, partly to act as an intermediary between the government and individual charities, and in 1951 it became the National Association, and continues to work on behalf of the interests of member charities. It acts in the architectural as well as the social interests of almshouses all over the country.

It was estimated soon after the War that the annual cost to the State of housing all the old people then accommodated in endowed almshouses would have been around eight million pounds. With nearly 30,000 people living in almshouses today, any present Chancellor of the Exchequer ought to be grateful to those benefactors of a 1,000 years whose gifts of money and property for the care of the aged have provided for the housing of so many.

Meanwhile, new almshouses have continued to appear, in spite of the Welfare State. At Glympton, Oxfordshire, single-storey houses with mullioned windows were built in 1949 with a coat of arms on the central gable, and at Horsham, West Sussex, a local firm designed the rebuilt St Mary's Almshouses in 1955, called by Pevsner 'depressingly genteel'. At Veryan, Cornwall, the Homeyard Homes were built in 1957 for the widows of Cornish seamen – a small estate containing two reproductions of the curious old round houses in the village, so built (according to legend) to keep the Devil out, by avoiding corners where he could lurk in wait.

New almshouses have been built in the last few years at Morcott in Leicestershire, and at Hounslow, to mention only two of the hundreds of projects for replacement and addition which are in progress every year to maintain old folk in accommodation of modern standards. New buildings are due to be erected at Congleton, Rawdon (West Yorkshire), Bromyard (Hereford and Worcester), Truro and Burnley; and rebuilding is scheduled or already under way at Thatcham (Berkshire), Patrington (Humberside) and Rawmarsh (South Yorkshire).

In the Northeast of England, modern industries have brought great crops of homes for their retired personnel, especially in Durham, Tyne and Wear and Cleveland, where the industrial towns and villages have their Aged Miners' Homes, all plain brick buildings except in odd cases where older houses have been taken over for the purpose.

In the Midlands, industries such as hosiery manufacture have long had their own almshouses such as the Framework Knitters' Cottage Homes in Leicester, and Edgar Corah's Charity at Loughborough.

The Department of the Environment makes grants for the maintenance of almshouse buildings which are of historic value, such as the sizeable Nicholas Chamberlaine Hospital at Bedworth in Warwickshire, built around 1840 in mock-Tudor style in brick, with a central chapel in the main range and wings with cloisters round a lawn. At Ackworth, West Yorkshire, the Georgian Mary Lowther Hospital, founded in 1741, is in process of restoration with a grant from the government.

The Society for the Protection of Ancient Buildings also makes grants to help restoration and preservation, whilst several charitable trusts help the less richly endowed foundations to meet the need for modern housing standards in their accommodation. In the older buildings, refurbishing accommodation can often mean very extensive repairs in dealing with the discovery of rotting timbers and death-watch beetle, and the need to comply with modern fire regulations and provide effective fire resistance.

Despite all this financial aid in keeping old and often very ancient foundations going more or less as their founders intended, it is, as David Owen wrote in *English Philanthropy, 1660–1960*, 'impossible to avoid the suspicion that the public sector is due to expand and the voluntary to contract, at least in a relative sense'. This is borne out, twenty-three years later, by the fact that there are now almshouses, offering free accommodation to old people, which have vacancies they are unable to fill. It is noticeable that vacancies occur mostly in establishments run by the Church, where there are often restrictions of movement, compulsory religious services and other rules and regulations – not to mention qualifications for entry – which might deter applicants in this changing society. The Welfare State, on the other hand, rightly takes care of the hard-up without imposing conditions on them, although it has to be said that the State's provision for old people is still not high on its list of priorities.

It is interesting to note, however, in spite of the foregoing, that in a league table of the top twenty most charitable towns in England, the old cathedral cities still hold their own. Omitting London, because its geographical limits cannot be sensibly defined in relation to the other cities mentioned, the table would be as follows, with the numbers of existing almshouse foundations in each:

Nottingham	29	Hereford	15
Birmingham	21	Hull	14
Bristol	19	Salisbury	13
Exeter	18	Cirencester	12

Canterbury	11	Derby	9
Cambridge	11	Worcester	9
Scarborough	11	Sheffield	9
King's Lynn	11	Maidstone	9
York	10	Watford	9
Newbury	10	Winchester	8

It is perhaps surprising that Nottingham so easily takes the honours. Birmingham's position is slightly eccentric, as a city which arose largely out of the approaching Industrial Revolution. It was only a country hamlet at the time of the Domesday Book, and only one charitable foundation is known of before the Tudor period. Clearly its almshouses grew as a response to increasing industrial poverty as the city grew to its present size, second only to London. Many of Nottingham's did, too, but the city already had a very respectable tradition of charity. The first known foundation was a lazar house under the patronage of the town in 1189, and it had six hospitals by the end of the fourteenth century, two of them under municipal administration. However we explain the positions of Nottingham and Birmingham in the list, other large modern industrial cities, such as Manchester, Leeds and Liverpool, are conspicuous by their absence.

After Nottingham and Birmingham, the list falls roughly into line with developments we have observed in previous chapters. If we look at the foundations in relation to the populations of the towns, however, the picture changes dramatically. The number of almshouse charities per thousand people in these *same twenty* towns and cities produces the following reshuffle:

Cirencester	1.0	Worcester	0.12
Newbury	0.41	Watford	0.11
Salisbury	0.37	Cambridge	0.11
King's Lynn	0.36	Nottingham	0.09
Canterbury	0.33	York	0.09
Hereford	0.32	Hull	0.04
Winchester	0.25	Bristol	0.04
Scarborough	0.25	Derby	0.04
Exeter	0.18	Birmingham	0.02
Maidstone	0.12	Sheffield	0.01

Here, the ancient cathedral cities do even better, and the towns of northern England even worse, than they did in the first table. But before we congratulate Cirencester on being the most charitable town in England, we should note, first, that one town's large almshouse accommodating, say, fifty old people, may more than equal another town's several smaller foundations in relation to population; and second, that on the basis of the second table, many of the towns and cities listed would lose their places in favour of smaller communities. For instance, Devizes would shoot straight into second place, and Abingdon and Hitchin would be hot on the heels of Hereford, even if we did not include some much smaller towns and villages which would certainly oust Cirencester from its leading position.

Nevertheless, the 'capital of the Cotswolds' clearly holds an honourable place in the story of English almshouses, the explanation lying, of course, in the wealth of its medieval wool merchants and the traditions they established in the town.

These statistics are not, however, to be taken too seriously, since all sorts of legitimate objections can be made to them. It may be unfair to stigmatize modern industrial towns for their lack of almshouses, because their rapid modern growth has been accompanied by prosperity which has not created a *need* for almshouses. Such towns as Huddersfield, Stoke-on-Trent and Salford have grown up in modern times with a social outlook entirely different from the old cathedral cities. And if we were to analyse towns and villages by the number of individuals housed in their charitable foundations, in relation to their populations, this would inevitably produce such eccentric results as to be almost meaningless.

One other significant fact ought to have an important place in any book on English almshouses. In the founding of such charities, women have always been men's equals. We have noticed buildings put up at the expense of some high-ranking ladies in the past – the duchesses of Marlborough and Somerset, for instance. But it is worth drawing attention to a few of the other almshouses founded by women, just to put them in the proper perspective. There are, still in existence, the Countess of Hardwicke's almshouses at Arrington, Cambridgeshire, the Countess of Derby's at Harefield and Viscountess Barrington's at Shrivenham. There are Dame Letitia Monson's almshouses at

Broxbourne, Dame Alice Leigh's at Stoneleigh, Dame Mary Yate's at Harvington; and Lady Peyton's at Isleham, Lady Dodd's at Ellesborough and Lady d'Arcy's at Colchester. Also Mrs Squire's at Walthamstow, Mrs Worthington's at Stilton and Mrs Dreyer's at Bungay; to say nothing of Miss Day's at Amersham, Miss Giles's at Chertsey and Miss Scotney's at Market Deeping. And there are a great many less formally named in honour of their female founders, such as Jane Cart at Dunstable, Louisa Powell at Ludlow, Catharine Ball at Cheltenham, Emma Simpson at Stockton-on-Tees, Lucy Brangwyn at Ditchling, Ann Routh at Beverley, Jessie Snow at Sleaford, Sarah Roope at Kingswear. These are only a few names picked at random out of many, but they make the point well enough.

Two of the scheduled *new* buildings mentioned earlier are of female foundation – the Evelyn Boscawen Trust at Truro, and Elizabeth Peel's Charity at Burnley – both venerable surnames in their respective areas.

Many modern almshouse groups, under the bureaucratic influence of the Charity Commission and local authorities, rejoice under cold and unimaginative titles like United Charities or Municipal Charities, but some, as we have seen, retain their quaint old names, and two such are in Devon. 'Yonder Corner Almshouses' at Ottery St Mary, and 'Eight Men of Broadclyst', proclaim in their names descriptive images that still seem to fit the purposes and the architecture of old almshouses better than the clinical titles so often bestowed on them by modern committees of accountants and councillors.

The romantic image of the almshouse remains that of white-haired old men and women living out their quiet lives, until the Iceman cometh, in peaceful cloistered surroundings where their every need is met, and where jackdaws stand sentinel on the old stone walls like the ghosts of former inmates seeing that the founder's intentions are not being flouted.

However anachronistic this picture might seem to some in the modern world of computerized Social Security and National Health, it will, happily be a long time yet before this thousand-year-old tradition of private provision for old people disappears entirely from the English scene.

An old gentleman at St Cross, Winchester, told me he counted it a privilege to spend his last days in such a place, and it was easy to see why. In the larger and wealthier ancient establishments, it is far more than just a matter of free lodging which appeals to many of the residents. The 'spirit of place' makes its mark on them. It is not so with all almshouses, of course, but all almshouses deserve respect as buildings which continue to serve an immensely useful purpose, and a large proportion of the older buildings also deserve our pride as treasures of our heritage of domestic architecture.

Select Bibliography

Aubrey, John. *Brief Lives*, Penguin, 1972
Birch, R. C. *The Shaping of the Welfare State*, Longman, 1974
Clay, R. M. *The Medieval Hospitals of England*, Methuen, 1909
Clifton-Taylor, Alec. *The Pattern of English Building*, Faber, 1972
Darley, Gillian. *Villages of Vision*, Architectural Press, 1975
Defoe, Daniel. *A Tour Through the Whole Island of Great Britain*, Penguin, 1971
Dickens, Charles. *The Uncommercial Traveller*, Everyman's Library edn., 1911
Garmonsway, G. N. (Ed.), *The Anglo-Saxon Chronicle*, Everyman's Library, 1972
Gay, John D. *The Geography of Religion in England*, Duckworth, 1971
George, M. Dorothy. *London Life in the Eighteenth Century*, Penguin, 1966
Godfrey, Walter H. *The English Almshouse*, Faber, 1955
Haley, K. D. H. *The Dutch in the Seventeenth Century*, Thames & Hudson, 1972
Heath, Sidney. *Old English Houses of Alms*, F. Griffiths, 1910
Hobson, J. M. *Some Early and Later Houses of Pity*, Routledge, 1926
Holmes, Mrs Basil. *The London Burial Grounds*, Fisher, Unwin, 1896
Jordan, W. K. *Philanthropy in England*, Allen & Unwin, 1959
Keating, Peter (Ed.). *Into Unknown England*, Fontana, 1976
Langland, William. *Piers the Ploughman*, Penguin, 1959
Martin, R. B. *Enter Rumour: Four Early Victorian Scandals*, Faber, 1962
Nuffield Foundation. *Old People*, Oxford University Press, 1947
Owen, David. *English Philanthropy, 1660–1960*, Harvard University Press, 1965
Pevsner, Nikolaus and others. *The Buildings of England* (46 vols.), Penguin, 1951–74
Pound, John. *Poverty and Vagrancy in Tudor England*, Longman, 1971
Tawney, R. H. *Religion and the Rise of Capitalism*, Penguin, 1961
Temple, Sir William. *Observations upon the United Provinces of the Netherlands*, Gregg International Publishers edition, 1971
Winckworth, Peter. *An Account of Almshouses*, London Association of Almshouses, 1948
Wood, Margaret. *The English Medieval House*, Dent, 1965
Youings, Joyce. *Sixteenth-Century England*, Penguin Books, 1984
Ziegler, Philip. *The Black Death*, Collins, 1969

Index